April 2017, I sit here in my beautiful Warwickshire apartment and look out over some of the finest countryside I have ever seen. A heart-warming seventy-second birthday party arranged by my loving family is just behind me and the warmth of the afternoon relaxes me into a reverie that encourages a host of memories from my past.

Might it be that other young people could find inspiration from hearing of the events that made me the person I am today?

I finally make the decision. I want my life story to be set down in print so that those coming behind me will learn something of the journey that has brought me to this peaceful and tranquil point in my life.

So, here it is Sonya's story.

Claire Sonya Garnett

04765

1

I dedicate this memoir to my beautiful and adorable step-Grandchildren:
Amelie, Theo, Zack, Taya, and Ruby.
Your love has enriched my life beyond measure.

This is *my* story

These are *my* words

I have spoken them *all*

But……….

My dear husband Alan has taken the words and moulded them into coherent prose. For this, he deserves full credit and my eternal gratitude.

Contents

The Assyrian Empire from 800 to 600 B.C.

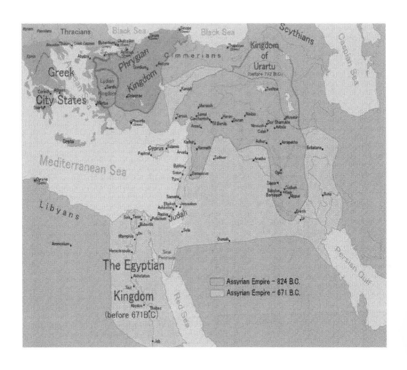

I

The Early Years

Kermanshah, Iran is where I was born on a chilly February morning in 1945. This comparatively small town lies about three hundred miles South West of Teheran and like most of ancient Persia has its share of relics and historic buildings. It has many famous sons from the field of Arts and Archaeology, and (somewhat surprisingly) was the birthplace of Doris Lessing, the internationally recognised author, and Nobel Prize, winner.

Before I describe my life, I feel it important to give a flavour of my roots and the cultural heritage and early influences that helped to mould my impressionable young self.

My father was a lorry driver and provided for the family that grew by the addition of my sister Bella and finally Joseph, my brother. I was taught that my Country – Iran – had, until recently been known as Persia. After all, it was only ten years before my birth that the Nazi regime in

Germany sought to influence Persian politics. They persuaded the Persian Government to instruct all of its embassies to propagate the name change to that of Iran. The close relationship of the word 'Iran' to *'Aryan'* was meant to demonstrate the racial purity of the Country. It would seem that Persia was anxious to preserve a friendly accommodation with the Nazis in the years leading up to WW2 because they complied immediately.

Although Iran is a great Muslim nation, we were not Muslims. My family and hundreds of families like us were Assyrians and therefore, Christian. Assyria, a hugely influential Country in Ancient Arabia resided in the triangle of the Euphrates and Tigris rivers and embraced parts of Persia, Turkey and some of what is now Iraq. Babylonia and its Hanging Gardens is probably a useful reminder of the cultural and geopolitical importance of this most ancient nation.

It is not a simple matter to adequately describe the history of Assyria. It is certainly true that the Assyrian language spawned both the Arabic and Farsi tongues and was also responsible for the foundation of the Greek language. The Assyrians of today are the descendants of the ancient Assyrian people, one of the earliest civilisations emerging in the Middle East, and have a history spanning at least six thousand, seven hundred years. From the earliest age, I was aware of the distinct cultural heritage of my people, and family gatherings always reinforced my understanding of the respectful harmony that prevailed whenever Assyrians were together.

At school, the spoken language was, of course, *Farsi* the native tongue of Iran, and as soon as we were home the only language spoken was Assyrian. Our family was completely fluent in both and, to this day, I am very pleased that, in addition to English, I can comfortably converse in either.

How everything might have changed if there had been a different outcome to an event which occurred on my second Birthday? My paternal grandfather smoked a somewhat odious pipe and, wishing to light up, had moved outside our home where everyone was gathered for my party. He had taken me with him and was watching me run around the path adjoining the house. He must have been distracted because suddenly everything was pandemonium when the teenage girl from next door burst into our home screaming that a woman in a black *chador*[1] had taken me away.

Everyone bolted outside and began challenging any woman they found dressed in such a way. It was several frantic minutes later that such a person was found, with me entirely shrouded inside her black garment. My Grandfather was apoplectic and screamed for her to release me. To everyone's astonishment, she shouted back just as loudly saying "this precious child is mine and you are trying to steal her from *me*."

This area of Kermanshah had but one part-time policeman, and he was soon on the scene. Apparently, he made it clear that he did not know which side to believe,

---

[1] A full-body-length cloak for women. Open at the front and worn over the head.

and a tense stand-off ensued. The deadlock was broken with the breathless arrival of my dear Grandmother Luba with whom I had an inseparable bond. Apparently, up to this moment I had been terrified and totally silent but, seeing her I exclaimed: "Nana Luba, Nana Luba" and this outburst completely satisfied the policeman who ordered the woman to return me immediately.

My Grandfather was asked if he wished to see the woman charged and he declined but only after terrifying her with a description of what he would do if she ever were seen in the area again.

Who is to say what might have happened if she had succeeded in stealing me that day. What would have been the impact on Mum, Dad, and Bella? Nana Luba doted upon me, and I can only imagine the effect of my abduction would have had on her. Many years later I was told that a lucrative market existed for toddlers at that time where they would be raised for prostitution or a slave-like existence as servants to wealthy families both in Iran and surrounding Countries.

*

Because of my Father's work, we moved to Hamadan when I was three. This town was a hundred miles or so closer to Teheran and affords me now some faint memories of Bazaars and shopping trips with my Mother. This was the first time I recall the pungent aroma of spices heaped on large wooden trays. I would cling to Mum's leg as she made her way through the busy shopping crowds only stopping to buy large purple aubergines. I also recollect an old man seated on a mat and presenting two very colourful snakes to passers-by. Another World indeed, but this was the World I was born into.

When I was five, we moved to an apartment in Teheran, The Capital city of Iran and this is where reliable recollections crowd my mind, and this is where my school life would begin a few years later. It was a very exciting city for me as a five-year-old. It was noisy, busy and simply full of traffic. I remember our apartment was small but adequate, and there was a generous courtyard behind the apartment block where we could play with other youngsters. We children slept in one small bedroom which was suffocatingly hot in the Summer but, overall, this was a happy period of my life.

Soon, it was time to prepare us for school. This decision was controversial within our family for Bella and me, being girls, prompted a huge row between my parents. Dad insisted that there was no point in sending girls to school and that only my younger brother Joseph should receive an education. Mum, who I remember being an equal match for my Dad in an argument, fiercely disagreed. This incident is seared upon my memory because of the severity of the disagreement that seemed to last for several days.

In fairness, it must be remembered that my Father had experienced a traumatic childhood. His Mother died when he was twelve and his Father, an unrepentant alcoholic, put him to work as an oil tanker driver's mate when he was just thirteen. There had been no opportunity for him to learn any form of parenting skills and while he was a kind man, he was not able to show us the parental love and interest that other fathers might have done in similar

11

circumstances. His background had taught him that only boys should get an education to prepare them for a lifetime of work and support of their family. For us girls to go to school then, was contrary to everything he knew about the struggles he felt would lay ahead for us all.

Dad's driving job often meant that he stayed away overnight due to the distances involved and despite such a serious argument, Mum took advantage of these times to secretly make our school uniforms. I should stress that she was no seamstress, and the elastic she used in the jumper sleeves cut unmercifully into our wrists. So much so that it caused our arms to swell; not an ideal way to start one's school life! I equally recall that Dad subsequently appeared to be resigned to defeat in this argument and life gradually returned to normal for us all. Never a man to show emotion, I believe he became proud of Bella and I as we began to demonstrate our capability to succeed at school.

Postwar Iran was a chaotic mix of inadequate Government structures and rudimentary local administration where literacy was often to be found wanting. I can best explain this bureaucratic nightmare by relating the circumstances that led to me being registered as Bella's *twin* when, in fact, I was her elder by thirteen months.

In 1945 there was conscription for all men of the appropriate age. To register my birth, both parents had, by law, to be present. My father, up to that time had been 'off the radar' for some reason and were he to attend for my registration then he would become 'known' to the authorities and immediately called into the armed forces for two years.

Such an eventuality would be devastating for our family as he could not possibly earn enough money to support us on the very meagre wage that conscripts received. Also, Assyrians in the military were relegated to the most menial tasks and he would almost certainly have become a servant to an Iranian Officer and would have been subject to his every whim for the next couple of years.   The midwife who delivered me was in no doubt whatsoever when she declared that I should remain unregistered. Mum and Dad agreed and so, officially, *I did not exist.*

In April the following year, Bella was born, and the same midwife assisted at her birth. By this time, the authorities had realised the folly of taking working-age fathers away from their families for two years, and an amnesty for such men had been declared. "Problem solved" declared the midwife. "Claire is a tiny infant, and so I shall record that I have today, delivered twins to Mrs Nargis Benjamin." And so it was that I was registered as Bella's twin sister the same day. One of the most prized possessions in our home was our Assyrian Bible which recorded all births and deaths. My birth was the first entry noted as *Claire Sonya born 22-02-1945.*

While this elegant solution solved Dad's problem, it created a heart-wrenching difficulty for me because it meant that I had to start school *the same day* as Bella. Pre-school education was unheard of in Iran at this time, and I endured a frustrating year waiting for my chance to begin my school life.   The teachers were comfortably satisfied that we were twins but, of course, I was now eight years old and had missed a complete year of school. I was desperate to learn, and my thirst for knowledge made the 'lost' year of my education incredibly frustrating to bear.

No account of our childhood in Teheran would be complete without reference to my Mother's abject failure to care for us properly. Dad was almost always away – sometimes for several days at a time – but this did not stop her leaving us alone for long periods while she went off - purportedly to meet with friends. At age six, she would leave me completely in charge of Bella and Joseph who was barely three years old.

Her lack of concern for our welfare was most dramatically demonstrated when a crushing coup d'état[2] was played out on the streets of Teheran in August 1953. Before lunch, Mum left the flat leaving me to get food for Bella and Joseph and to make sure they got into no trouble. She made it clear that she would be back no later than four in the afternoon. As the day wore on, there was a considerable increase in sounds of violence down in the street. I could see large tanks moving past with groups of armed men following closely behind. The staccato rattle of gunfire filled me with dread, and I fully expected armed intruders to burst in at any moment.

---

[2] In August 1953 Prime Minister Mohammad Mossadegh attempted to Nationalise the Anglo-Iranian oil Company (now BP). He was overthrown in a coup allowing Mohammad Reza Pahlavi (The Shah of Iran) to assert his position as King. A function he carried out for the next 25 years.

It was now nearly five o'clock and no sign of Mum; I could not stop shaking with fear. What should I do? Try to act as normal was all I could think and so I bathed Joseph in the small metal tub in the kitchen and put him to bed. Bella was too young to appreciate what was happening and continued to play with her toys.

Six o'clock now, and I was completely sure that Mum had been killed in the fighting. I lay on the uncarpeted portion of the floor with my ear to the boards. I had learned from previous scares that, by doing this, I could hear Mum's footsteps before she reached the front door. I could not stop crying. What was I to do if she were dead? Dad was not due back for two more days, and it looked to me as though we had been invaded by a foreign power.

Finally, at half-past-six, Mum returned, a little flustered by the revolutionary activity in the City but completely unrepentant about the hours of terror her feckless behaviour had subjected me to. After that, I was often to be the 'responsible adult' in our family even though I was only eight as Mum continued in her selfish and reckless behaviour. This was the first day in my life when I realised that I could never depend on others to shelter me from life's storms and that I had better become fully independent without delay.

'Proper school' in Iran started at age seven, and it was on 'our' seventh birthday that we began at the Shahnaz Pahlavi School. This establishment is named after the Shah's first daughter. It was an Iranian school save for four Assyrian girls - myself, Bella and two others - plus two Jewish girls. The six of us joined in all classes but were excused religious education.

Apart from impossibly tight sleeves In our jumpers, Mum created another, more serious difficulty when she prepared our first packed lunch. It had been made clear that no food would be provided for pupils at midday and so She had made a perfect lunch for Bella and me. She did not own anything that resembled a lunchbox, and so she emptied one of Dad's tin boxes that he often used in place of a toilet bag while away on his travels. Every piece of food was impregnated with the taste of soap, and it was too much for our young stomachs to bear. It was not long before we were both sick much to the fascination of the other first-day pupils.

Despite these first-day setbacks, I loved school, and both Bella and I regularly scored near the top of the class at the end of term exams. My handwriting was considered above the average, and I was deputed to write various messages on the blackboard when required. For this, I was made a Prefect, a rank that followed me in each subsequent year. I remember the teachers being sincere and very helpful, and I began to enjoy school life in Teheran very much indeed.

The school lunch period was two hours at midday and children mostly went home for their meal. As we had no transport to get home, we relied upon Mum's packed lunches to see us through the day. I well remember the four children of a high-born Persian family who also stayed at school during lunchtime. Each day, a chauffeur would bring a hot lunch to them. As soon as he left, these children would eagerly seek us out, and we would exchange meals.

We were delighted to sample such delicacies as hot Persian kebabs and, khoresht-e badnjan (Aubergine Stew), and they to have Assyrian dolmas, red rice and other delights that they had never tasted before.   Needless to say, we were fully accepted by the Persian majority and never, ever felt like the small minority that we clearly were.

I am sure that most people will look back and feel that school moulded them in some way. For me, the consistent and genuine interest from my teachers was truly motivating, which is why my memory of this period all these years later, is so crystal clear.

Religion at school did not seem to be a very significant part of our education, and certainly, there was no hint of the feverish zealotry that seized the Country after The Shah was deposed many years later. It was the custom in school for us to have the same - always female - teacher every school day for a complete year. I will never forget being summoned to the staff room when I was eleven and being confronted with the news that I was to present myself to my teacher's home the next morning before school. "You are not to worry Claire, she needs you to help her with something. Be sure not to be late." Luckily, I knew where she lived as I passed her house each day on my way to school.

Despite being told not to worry about the visit, I still arrived the next morning with considerable trepidation. I nearly cried with relief when she welcomed me warmly and invited me in. She gave me a detailed tour of her kitchen explaining that she was preparing several dishes for a party that evening.   She then astonished me by saying that *I was to be in charge of food cooking throughout the day.* She would telephone me at the end of each school lesson for an update, or to give me further instruction.

She made it clear that the Headmistress not only knew of this arrangement but approved it warmly, as they both saw this as part of my education. She then left me alone and went off to school. I remember being nervous but also being proud beyond belief that I had been chosen for this task ahead of the other forty girls in our class. She did contact me several times in the day and, under her tutelage, I cooked, skinned and diced a calf's tongue ready for a Russian Salad that evening.

When she came home, she was so pleased with what I had done - every utensil washed and put away - that she invited me to stay for the first hour of the party. Never was an eleven-year-old prouder or more inspired by the confidence this caring teacher had shown in me. My feet hardly touched the ground as I walked home from her house. I think this character building exercise could only have happened in pre-revolution Iran and would be inconceivable here within our formulaic Western educational system.

*

As my story will show, dancing was to become a very significant part of my life from my teen years onwards, and family lore attributes this to my Aunty Doris. When I was four, she took me, for a very special treat, to the cinema where we saw a film featuring *Samia Gamal*, an internationally celebrated Belly Dancer. When we returned home, I grabbed my small toy tambourine and did my best to emulate the renowned dancer I had just seen. Soon, a small replica costume had been made and, after that, I was the main attraction at family gatherings.

We were very fortunate in Teheran to have a Russian lady called *Madam Lilly* as a leading light in amateur theatrics designed to illuminate our heritage. *Madam Lilly* was a renowned Assyrian intellectual whose reputation made her a significant force within Teheran's Assyrian community. Noticing that there was not much to do for children outside of school hours she had formed an Assyrian youth group designed to recognise and foster creative talent from those willing to attend.

My cousin was a member of this group which, not surprisingly given the conservative nature of life at this time, was very short of girls to play parts in the little playlets which were being performed. *Madam Lilly* made an appeal to all members of the group, and thus it was that Bella and I, just entering our teenage years, found ourselves part of her entourage.

Although Assyrians were a tiny minority in Iran, they were given a weekly one-hour slot on local TV so that their culture could be sustained. By now, it was known within the group that I could dance, and *Madam Lilly* proposed that I perform my little routine on live TV. I was terrified and excited in equal measure, but the live musicians playing traditional Assyrian folk music gave me the courage I needed. I had just had my fourteenth birthday and was far from confident expressing myself in public but, I am pleased to say, there were some complimentary calls to the TV station following my appearance, and so it was, a few months later, I was invited back to perform my dance once again.

2

My wonderful Nana Luba

My story would never be complete unless I explained the profound influence that my maternal grandparents had upon me. I was truly blessed to have Grandpa and Nana Luba in my life. Grandpa was born of a distinguished Assyrian family and had a reputation as a fluent speaker and writer of the original Assyrian language. They had a restaurant in Kermanshah during the Second World War, and it was popular with both Muslims and Christians alike as Nana Luba was a well-respected cook in the area. It was also a favourite venue for the many English Managers of British Petroleum, who had massive refinery operations nearby since Grandpa made no secret of his admiration for all things British.

As the war progressed, Germany increasingly asserted itself towards Iran, and Grandpa found himself under very restrictive House Arrest by the Iranian military as possibly a British spy, but certainly a British sympathiser. It was said that his dignity and bearing led to his eventual release, but this frightening experience confirmed him as a passionate Anglophile after that.

The strictures of confinement and the unpleasant treatment meted out to him while imprisoned led to him becoming very ill with kidney problems, and the restaurant business failed as a result. His illness was an absolute disaster as he and Nana Luba needed to sell *literally everything* to pay for the considerable cost of his treatment. With all their possessions sold, the last item to go was Nana's sewing machine.

A stranger had come to buy it and had paid her the money. As he moved to lift it, I started to scream and desperately tried to stop him. I was only two, but I am told the dramatic scene I created was very considerable. To this day, I cannot explain my frantic behaviour. I was certainly aware of the importance of the machine to Nana Luba and can only think that its removal was akin to a part of her being taken away. Certainly, my wailing was sufficient for the man to become disconcerted and, putting the machine back in its place, he declared that my outburst was a bad omen for him. He insisted that Nana Luba kept both the machine *and the money* as it was plain to see how vital sewing was to the family.

Nana Luba immediately took up sewing and garment making for people in the neighbourhood from which she made enough money to feed them both and buy extra medical help for Grandpa. Once his health had recovered, they looked for another opportunity to open a restaurant which they eventually did in a small town called a Sahneh just outside Kermanshah.

This location was strategically vital to Grandpa since all the oil tankers from the Kermanshah refinery had to pass through this village on their way to Teheran. The drivers all knew Nana Luba and Grandad from their first restaurant and made sure to stop and enjoy their food once more.

When my family moved to Teheran, we three children would be sent back to Sahneh each year to spend the long summer months with my Grandparents. They had an orchard in which we would play day after day. I fondly remember a small waterfall set in an idyllic valley where, with my cousins, we would be allowed to lead a donkey carrying all the provisions needed for memorable picnics. Every day we ate excellent food from their restaurant and because of the heat, slept outside on its flat roof every night. Those nights sleeping out in the open remain a vivid recollection. Countless stars crowded the night sky, and I would be mesmerised by the breath-taking celestial display. Early morning too was fascinating from my lofty viewpoint. I could look over the town as the first fingers of dawn brought other buildings into focus. It was quiet save for the occasional bark of a dog, and I would watch with interest as women began to emerge from their homes to put out washing and to air bedding in advance of the heat of the day to come. Such tranquillity just before the town shook itself awake was both awe-inspiring and memorable.

One such night of roof-top slumber, however, gave us an experience of unparalleled excitement and fear. Bella, Joseph and I were extremely restless under our mosquito nets as the nighttime temperature was still brutal. In the restaurant garden beneath us, several oil-tanker drivers were sleeping under mosquito screens on folding wooden cots provided by my Grandad. The popularity of Nana Luba's Assyrian food made this a very desirable overnight stop for lorries making their way to Teheran and the

23

garden was invariably occupied through the night by a significant group of well-fed customers.

For the extraordinary events of the next few hours to have proper context, I should first describe a small, very well run, health clinic just two hundred metres away from the restaurant. It had been set-up shortly after the end of the war by a married German couple in their forties. It was said that they were horrified by the Nazi cruelty they had witnessed in the previous decade and had determined to bring their medical skills - he was a doctor and she a senior nurse - to rural Iran. Medical facilities were very sparse in Sahneh, and they soon had developed a busy and thriving practice. They were both strikingly blonde and spent all their spare time at Grandpa's restaurant since they both spoke excellent English – as did my Grandparents - and no one in the area spoke German. They both were to play a pivotal role in the events that unfolded during this fateful night.

The first light of dawn had just appeared when I was woken violently by such a volume of shouting as I had never before experienced. I could hear my Grandpa screaming "get them inside. Get them all inside!" This instruction, I presumed, was directed at Nana Luba.

Peering over the side of the flat roof I became aware of people running in all directions. The ladder which we used to get up to the flat roof was leaning at a generous angle against the wall, and I was horrified to see Grandpa run towards it and throw it to the ground with one swipe of his arm. Moving to the other side, I looked over to see the sleeping drivers being roughly roused by a man I had never seen before.   Were we being attacked?   Robbers were not unknown in the area but would they confront so many able-bodied men? I looked back at Bella and Joseph both of whom still appeared to be sleeping and wondered what, if anything, I should do.

At that moment, an animal-like howling pierced the air with an intensity which seemed to my young ears to last forever. Once more I ran to the other side of the roof and looked over to see a sight that I shall never forget. A farmer, who I recognised from the adjoining small-holding was standing over a huge dog which he had impaled with a five-pronged metal hay fork. The animal was obviously quite dead. This must be it then, a mad dog but why was there still so much panic beneath me? I had barely enough time to absorb the remarkable scene before I saw Grandpa, in his pyjamas, with a *wheelbarrow* in which was slumped one of the overnight guests. With a massive effort, he was running it towards the German clinic. Sometime later, we were brought down and kept in the small lounge next to the dining area. Explanations there were none, but I was acutely aware of the horror-stricken faces of the adults that we saw that morning.

And finally, the story was told. A sizeable – Mastiff-type-dog belonging to a shepherd in the hills above us was rabid. It had attacked and subsequently killed, two farm employees before descending during the night. It had bitten three of our sleeping residents – one of whom later died – and Grandpa was hailed as a hero because he managed to get the other two to the clinic using the only transport he had – his garden wheelbarrow. Very quickly a small team from Teheran visited the restaurant and

25

removed the dog's head for forensic examination. They then supervised the fire which was used to destroy the remains of this sick animal. As soon as rabies was confirmed, another team visited our district and, as a precaution, set about culling every dog in the neighbourhood. Very unfortunately, this included Grandpa's faithful sheepdog, Ben. This brave creature had confronted the crazed animal and received a significant bite to his leg as a result. To see the most loved male adult in my life weep with the pain of this decision burned my young heart in a way that was entirely new to me.

*

In retrospect, it was Grandpa's orchard that gave me my very first exposure to the effect of drugs as opium was very widely used then in Iran and smoking a Hookah pipe was not at all uncommon.

The farm next door to Grandad's orchard grew beautiful apples, and although our orchard had them as well, those on his land were for us a much-prized flavour. About four o'clock each afternoon, *Ali Abbas*, the farmer, would take a break by having tea and a smoke of opium. From our concealed position, we would watch him load his pipe with a sticky ball of opium and relax in the sun. Very soon he would nod off and often we would see his long beard dip into the teacup. This was our signal to creep in and help ourselves to his excellent tasting apples.

Grandpa found a novel way of paying us a little pocket money by buying the cherries that we picked in his orchard. Cleverly, he made weighing scales out of cleaned and polished *Cherry Blossom* tins and would solemnly negotiate a price with us each evening.

Across the road from Grandpa's restaurant was a Persian cafe. I was very interested in the food they served there and one day plucked up the courage to ask Grandpa if he could buy me a meal from them. I had saved all my 'cherry money' and eagerly offered it all to him so that he could make this purchase. The owner of the cafe was apparently so moved by my wish to sample Persian cuisine, that he heaped a plate with all the delicacies on their menu and refused to take any money. It was delicious, but this six-year-old ate only about ten per cent of the huge platter!

It was about this time that Nana Luba began quietly to teach us the essential elements of moral behaviour. She guided us in such matters as fairness, compassion and personal dignity. Her gentle kindness affected me profoundly and, even as a young six-year-old, I vowed that I would try to emulate her in every way when I was grown up. Even now, I think of her most days, and her wisdom still informs many of my decisions.

*

Although this is a memoir of *my* life, I feel compelled to say a little about the struggles that Assyrians encountered in years gone by and can best illustrate this by relating the unbearable experience of my Grandparents when they were young.

Nana Luba was born around 1905 to an Assyrian couple who worked a small farm in Persian Azerbaijan. The First

World War wreaked carnage in this area as the Ottoman Empire swept all before it in its attempt to invade and occupy Persia. Their farm was eventually overrun by marauding forces bent on the genocide of any Christians, and Nana Luba's mother and father were killed by being thrown down their well. Nana, who was then twelve and her two brothers had been hidden by near- neighbours who later took them to a convent for safety. There, Christian nuns took care of them for the next year and began to teach them English.

Not far away lived another Assyrian family of Russian extraction. They were somewhat distinguished since each of the four brothers was either a scientist, engineer or similar professional status and, by luck, they had avoided the rampaging army that swept through the region. Grandpa, the second of the brothers, who was born around the turn of the Century approached the convent knowing that only Christian souls would reside there. He asked if he could formally introduce himself to the Assyrian girl 'Luba.' It seems that the nuns were very pleased with this possible betrothal but stipulated that Grandpa would have to take Luba's two brothers as part of the deal. This he did, and after getting married, they moved to Kermanshah where their first-born was my Mother Nargis.

Nana told me this story when I was about thirteen and only then because I badgered her to recount details of her early life. The dignified way she recalled the unspeakable terror of that time has left me with an indelible memory of this most graceful and generous-hearted lady. It is impossible to comprehend how young children survived horrors such as this and how sad it is, one hundred years later, that such barbaric savagery continues to be a daily currency in the war-torn Middle East.

I would sit with Nana when I was very young while she was busy making garments for Grandpa and the family. She often pretended to need my help, and I was then allowed to turn the wheel of her old *Singer* sewing machine. I spent hours watching her skillfully create items of clothing and soon I was sewing small pieces of fabric myself. I know that this 'apprenticeship' at such a young age was fruitful since, at age ten, I was asked by Dad to make something for him. He had long wished to own a 'cowboy type' shirt with a bold check pattern. Using all that I had learned, I made the shirt for him, and he wore it for several years while away on his trips. This project was not without challenge since I was not tall enough to work the foot treadle of the Singer machine and could only manage it if I *stood up* while sewing.

*

To explain the events which later overtook Grandpa and Nana Luba I must break from my chronological record of family events to describe the political earthquake, caused by The Shah's removal, which so traumatised the majority of the Iranian population.

The eventual fall of the Shah had a catastrophic effect on everyday life in Iran, particularly for non-Muslims. In 1980 Grandpa's valuable local connections finally helped him and Nana Luba flee Iran for America. Of course, they were not able to convert any of their assets to cash before they had to leave for Modesto, California. As a consequence, their life after that was spartan indeed, but I was by then able to help them a little, and they both passed away peacefully in 1985.

The overthrow of the Shah, swiftly followed by the much-heralded return of Ayatollah Khomeini, dashed any faint hopes that I might one day return to the Country of my birth.   I grew up in a liberal and enlightened Iran. Certainly, the Shah was capable of much cruelty, always ensuring that key National and Regional functions were fulfilled by members of his extended family. Despite this dictatorial approach to Government, there was a relaxed and good-humoured atmosphere within communities during this period where generous concern for one's neighbour was the norm.

Comparing this to the over-zealous religious extremism that accompanied the Khomeini era leaves older Iranians pining for a return to pre-revolution days.   It is almost incomprehensible for a Westerner to fully appreciate what life under the Mullahs is like, but the oppression – particularly of women and girls – is a suffocating burden that is a daily experience for everyone.

Now, I must return to the story of my family.

At the end of the Second World War, My father had an established job driving tanker lorries for *British Petroleum,* something he was still doing when I was born. Little did I realise as a small child how my father's driving skill would later come to completely transform the lives of the whole family.   My mother, Nargis was, by all accounts a local 'beauty' in the area but she had no formal education since girls were not sent to school in pre-war Iran. As she was an Assyrian however, she had the Christian credentials to be an appropriate match for my Dad, and, after a semi-formal introduction at a carefully engineered house party, they eventually married.

I have learned from family members that we were, in every respect, an average family and that there was always food on our table. It would seem that my Grandfather's social status as a successful restaurateur made our lives somewhat more comfortable since it was clear that raising a family in Kermanshah in the late 1940s was anything but easy. Without a doubt, our move to Teheran improved life for us all, and we seemed to be comfortably settled. That is until an Irishman called Paddy made contact with Dad a few weeks after my thirteenth Birthday………..

3

How Coincidences shape lives

I am a fatalist. Many events in my life have convinced me that some seeming coincidences are pre-determined or, at the very least are persuasive markers that it would be folly to ignore. The following catalogue of 'coincidences' completely altered the destiny of myself and my family and they began at my Grandad's restaurant in Sahneh.

A local customer brought in an Irishman whose single-decker British coach had broken down nearby. Paddy did not speak a word of Farsi, but Grandad spoke passable English and offered his help. Paddy had converted the bus to a motorhome and was accompanied by his wife on this exploration holiday. He explained that he was thinking of starting a business running overland trips from London to Bombay, which, bearing in mind this was 1958, was both ground-breaking and adventurous. Grandad had soon located a Leyland dealer, and the spare parts were ordered to arrive at the restaurant the following day.

Grandad and Nana Luba insisted that Paddy and his wife stay the night in their home rather than in their coach. Moreover, when the parts arrived, Grandad would accept no payment at all insisting it was an honour to meet an English speaking, gentleman. Paddy was overwhelmed with this generosity and begged for an opportunity to repay the kindness shown to him. As it happened, Grandad's second daughter Doris – my Mother's sister – was staying at the restaurant for a few days. Grandad said if Paddy would take her back to our home in Teheran as he passed through, then this would be ample recompense.

This significant coincidence meant that, later in the day, Paddy was knocking on our door and introducing both he and his wife. This first contact with us was not without difficulty since Paddy had no knowledge of our language and we certainly spoke no English. But, such is the way with Assyrian courtesy, my Mother insisted they join us for a meal as my Father was not due home for a couple of hours. Dad had a real facility with languages. Apart from English, he spoke Farsi, Assyrian, Turkish and Pashto and was even able to converse in the unique dialect of some of the Iranian hill tribes. Additionally, Dad was a skilled motor mechanic who specialised in engine maintenance, and I am sure that this fact alone made him someone of significant interest to Paddy.

When Dad arrived home, they were soon in deep conversation, and it was not long before Paddy had suggested that Dad joined him as a driver when the new business was up and running. Paddy took lots of photos of us all and, with this new friendship firmly established, promised to make contact once he had returned to England. We heard nothing for about eight months and had reluctantly decided that Paddy had been less than sincere when a package finally arrived. It contained a large number of beautiful photographs he had taken while he was with us and, most importantly, a firm offer of employment for Dad.

I should perhaps pause here to explain that most, if not all Assyrians secretly hoped they could leave Iraq/Iran and relocate to a Christian country. It was not that there was discrimination against us, it was just a wish to live in a Christian, rather than Muslim society.

My Mother, ever eager to best her Assyrian neighbours, was passionate about Paddy's job offer. She pushed Dad relentlessly to accept the invitation since a condition of the offer was that the whole family would move to England. If this happened, then Mum's bragging rights in the local Assyrian community would know *no bounds*. It was not possible in Iran at that time to apply for a passport unless one had a *formal offer of work* abroad. That is why Paddy's employment offer was invaluable to this average, typical Teheran family. Dad at once set about procuring the necessary permissions for the family to immigrate to the U.K. but Iranian Bureaucracy was both convoluted and antiquated, and it took six months for him to secure the necessary passports and U.K. visas.

In 1959, Paddy made his first fare-paying overland expedition from London to Bombay. The journey took about three months, and his thirty passengers were hardy souls that I can best describe as 'stoically British.' Paddy brought the bus to us in Teheran, and we all said goodbye to Dad, who joined Paddy and then shared the driving for the rest of the Journey to Bombay. This overland adventure was truly ground-breaking, and the following warning, an original *India Man* brochure from that time, sums up what it was that passengers should expect.

The India Man Company

WARNING

We have always been at great pains to STRESS that this journey is an 'EXPEDITION' rather than a 'TOUR' in the normal sense. IT IS NOT - the MOST COMFORTABLE WAY OF TRAVELLING. IT IS NOT - the CHEAPEST WAY OF TRAVELLING. It is a rugged, rewarding journey that will take you across mountains and deserts and into the remotest parts of some very primitive countries.

It will bring you into the company of people who are warm, 'happy go lucky', tolerant and human - so if there is any 'gingerbread' in your make up, better stay away! Bluntly - it is a trip for the genuine TRAVELLER rather than the modern TOURIST. Luxury does not exist all along the overland route. Hotels range from excellent to pretty putrid but all are endurable and if you can rise above the limitations of 'creature comforts' you will certainly enjoy this trip.

OUR WARNING IS NO STUNT - so please - please - for your sake, for our sake, for God's sake! - stay away if you want mollycoddling.

We didn't see much of Dad for the next year and a half as he was always on the road with Paddy. It was evident to us teenage children that Mum could be a harridan, and I heard tell that he was pleased to be away working. In 1960 however, he got the ultimatum from Mum – "move us to England *or else*" So it was, then that we began the process of leaving Iran forever.

Schools in Iran closed for three months in Summer because of the extreme heat and the remaining nine months were without another break. I was now thirteen and very bored with such a long holiday which is why I approached a local tailor shop and asked if they needed an apprentice. The Assyrian owner was delighted and took me on immediately at the same pay rate as the male assistants. It was thrilling. I was doing something at which I was useful, and earning more money than ever before, and I was acquiring new garment making skills each day.

The three months passed in a blur and my mind was already turning to a similar post the following year, but I was not prepared to return to the same shop. My reluctance stemmed from the fact that the owner was, quite simply, a dirty old man. When ladies came in for fittings, he would always take a position so that he could watch them while they were changing behind a modesty curtain. He would manage to touch them inappropriately when adjusting their dresses and, on several occasions, we saw him look up their skirt when he was behind them. I loved the work, however, and the money was excellent, so I made up a story that my parents would not allow me to work in a shop during holidays the following year. Could he recommend anyone that I could approach? He told me of an Assyrian lady dressmaker to private clients who operated from her apartment on the same road, and I visited her later that day. She was delighted to agree that I could spend the next Summer with her at the same pay.

So it was the following year that I began to acquire the skills of bespoke dressmaking. I was never so happy. Hardly a day would pass when I had not learned a new technique, and the pay was allowing me for the first time, to be able to buy some things of my own.

February 1960 found each of us packed and ready to leave. Our clothes were stuffed into every case we could find, but nothing else could travel with us for want of space on Paddy's bus. Bella and I were desperately sad. We loved school, we had lots of friends, and I had guaranteed work each Summer. We hated the idea of leaving Teheran for good and considered our parents as thoughtless and cruel to wrench us away from everything we loved.

The atmosphere in the bus was very subdued, and a few quiet tears were being shed. Paddy must have been aware of this since he made a detour after leaving Teheran and drove us due North to the Caspian Sea so that we children could marvel at our first ever sight of an ocean. The mood in the bus lifted considerably after such a wondrous sight.

The journey took us North West through Turkey, Istanbul, Bulgaria and Yugoslavia until we finally reached Austria. We children were tired but very, very happy and especially thrilled that Paddy had negotiated with the owner of a small hotel at *Fuschl-am-See* for us all to stay for three months. This little Austrian municipality had only one thousand five hundred inhabitants and nestled at the edge of a lake between Salzburg and Bad Ischl. The surprising decision for us to stay here was necessary since no arrangements had been made for our arrival in England. There was yet accommodation to organise and visas to secure. Thus, it was that Dad and Paddy (plus all the other fare-paying passengers) continued to London without us.

Austria was a revelation with green and lush countryside nestling next to picture-perfect lakes. It could not have been a greater contrast to the Iranian home we had left such a short while ago.   I began to pick up the rudiments of the German language and – at age fifteen - began to notice boys for the first time. The wife of the hotel owner invited me to use her sewing machine which enabled me to make Western-style summer dresses for myself and Bella, and we suddenly felt very grown up. It was blissful Summer weather, and the kindness showed to us by everyone at the hotel only added to the happiness we all felt.

We spent many hours beside the lake staring with envy at the collection of rowing boats being rented out to visitors by a local man called Werner.   Over-time, he became friendly towards us and probably had realised that we had no money whatsoever. With a mixture of hand signals and basic German, he made us an offer of employment. When visitors returned the rowing boats, they were left in a disorganised melee at the mooring point.   If we would return each boat to the covered boathouse area, then we could have a boat for the three of us without charge. We were ecstatic. His rowing boats had never been so tidily arranged, and we spent hours on the lake living out the fanciful adventures that the endless sunshine and crystal-clear water inspired in three very suggestible Assyrian children.

Any nostalgia we had for Teheran was fading fast, and it was, therefore, with a tinge of regret that, after three incredibly happy months, the time came for us to leave. Paddy duly arrived in a large estate car to take us on the final leg of our marathon journey to England.

4

And so, to England

It is not easy to describe the impact of this extraordinary relocation from our apartment and school in Teheran to Kingston-upon-Thames Surrey. None of us spoke a word of English, and although Dad had given Mum money, he was off once more on his travels, and we had to fend for ourselves. My brother was soon accepted into a local school, and I can only imagine how tough this must have been for an eleven-year-old who had no knowledge of English. Bella and I never went to school since it quickly became apparent that Dad had made no arrangements for either of us.

I desperately wished to go to school in England. I had succeeded well at my school in Teheran and wanted to continue my education and importantly, learn English. The local schools were just not prepared to take a fifteen-year-old girl who did not have any knowledge of the language. Mum was no help whatsoever and was busy spending the money Dad had left us on mostly useless and self-indulgent items.

I finally turned to Paddy's wife who was very understanding and introduced me to a Mrs Edlin, who was involved in a recruitment agency. She found me a placement as an au pair in Claygate not far from our new Kingston home. This was a frightening introduction to British life for me since I was required to be up at six am every morning to polish shoes for both the husband and wife plus four children. I had to cook breakfast for everyone, clean the large house each day and take care of the four school kids until it was time for bed. After clearing up all the dinner things behind the husband and wife, I was allowed to go to my room at about nine-thirty each night. As a fifteen-year-old, I was physically incapable of sustaining this slave-like existence, and I just had to leave after two weeks.

Back at the recruitment agency, I explained that I was an experienced dressmaker but, without a machine, I could do nothing. This gave the kindly Mrs Edlin an ingenious idea. She would talk to her friends to see if any of them would like me to make clothes for them *in their own home.* A short time later I found myself in Leatherhead, in the grand detached house of a retired fashion model, making dresses for her in one of the many spare bedrooms. The house was magnificent, and I was awestruck by both the spaciousness and the elegant furnishings. I had *never* seen anything to match this home, and it left a lasting impression upon my teenage mind.

Everything worked well, and she was delighted with my skill and speed of work. It was not long before she asked if she could bring a friend to the house as she would also like to have a dress made. Soon, I was making clothes for her and three of her friends and was quietly enjoying the praise being given for my work.

I kept in regular contact with Mrs Edlin who was very impressed with my growing business in Leatherhead. Although I was being paid fairly, she was confident that I could build a viable dressmaking business with the right help. After a very positive chat in her office, she offered to set me up in her home to make garments on a professional basis. She committed to spreading the word about me and, in return, would take fifteen per cent of my earnings. With her help, I put together a simple one-sheet mailshot and delivered it to every prestigious house in the wealthy local neighbourhood of Coombe Hill.

The results were nothing short of astonishing, and I was flooded with work. Customers would meet me at Mrs Edlin's house for fittings, and the business grew quickly. I would work away in the spare room, and Mrs Edlin would bring me boiled eggs and 'Marmite soldiers' for my lunch – a wonderful introduction to English cuisine. I made ball gowns, bridal outfits, smart holiday wear and many ladies' business suits and, at last, I was earning money and fulfilling my most urgent dream of signing up for evening classes at Kingston's *Tiffin school*. The course *'English for Foreign Students'* was just what I needed. I tried to attend every single night although this wasn't always possible, but I was quickly getting an understanding of correct, Basic English.

One of my first dressmaking clients was a truly beautiful lady called *Linda Fairclough* who had just been crowned

Miss UK 1960. My joy at meeting her was not just confined to her radiant beauty but also her *perfect figure.* Most of my dressmaking skills had hitherto been reserved for dressing ladies of significantly varied sizes and shapes, but here I was working with *the perfect* mannequin silhouette. She arrived accompanied by a gentleman who proceeded to show me some leopard-skin print fabric. He explained that they required a tight-fitting dress to be made "as low at the top as possible and as high from the bottom as decent." I set to work and soon had the dress completed. They returned, and Miss Fairclough slipped it on. The effect was *astonishing.* She looked stunning. I was utterly proud of my work since it fitted perfectly. To say they were delighted was an understatement. They hugged one another and then they hugged me. The man paid me the six-pound fee plus *an incredible* four-pound tip. Happy clients for sure but an even more delighted dressmaker on this occasion.

During this period, Bella had also been placed as an au pair but this lasted only two months, and she was soon back home with nothing to do. We both realised that we had to earn money to keep our family together as Mum, blinded by the relatively good life of Kingston, was proving to be hopeless with household budgeting. Bella said she wanted to get into hairdressing but seemed unable to realise this wish for herself. On one of my rare days off, I walked around Kingston and went to every hairdresser asking if they needed an apprentice. I was turned down at each save that the last one told me a sister shop in Bayswater London was looking for someone. I made contact immediately and got Bella a placement. She was delighted, but it was tough for her because of the long journey each day required two buses each way. She now had a secure job, however, and life for us all began to take a distinct turn for the better.

My best dressmaking client was a certain Mrs Fedder whose husband owned a chain of Chemist shops. She kept me very busy making a great variety of outfits since she and her husband frequently took cruise holidays. Looking back, I am aware that Mrs Fedder was the first real friend that I had and her visits for fittings often extended into long chats about her family and mine. She wanted to know why it was that I was sitting on my own, in a stranger's house, sewing garments when I could have a regular job elsewhere? I assured her there was nothing I would have liked more but I was in England on a Visitor's Visa and did not have a Work Permit. Demonstrably shocked at this bar to my progress she invited me home to meet her husband.

"I am sure he can get you a Work Permit, and you can work in one of his shops." She later admitted that she felt somewhat sorry for my 'sweatshop' existence in Mrs Edlin's spare bedroom and thought I could do much better for myself. She also made no secret of the fact that she was matchmaking me with her seventeen-year-old Son Graham.

Mr Fedder readily offered me a position in his Queensway London shop in the knowledge that this could not happen for six months since that was the time it would take me to finish my existing dressmaking orders. The salary and regularity of the work he was proposing were appealing, and the whole family was showing me such kindness that I happily accepted. Not long after this, the staff of Mr Fedder's eight shops had their Christmas party and – to my surprise and delight – I received an invitation.

I was *so* excited. I set about making myself a white crepe de Chene party dress and literally counted down the days before the event. I had never before been to a party such as this, but everyone was full of fun and very kind towards me. I was painfully aware how little English I had, but no one seemed to be concerned. Mrs Fedder made a point of introducing me to Graham who seemed initially to be somewhat nervous. He paid me a lot of attention, though, and I must say that I was very taken both with his good looks and boyish charm. He plucked up the courage to tell me that he had seen me arrive for my interview several weeks before and had set his heart upon asking me out.

Graham's brother Brian was also at the party. He was nineteen and engaged to Valerie, a very attractive girl who – although she was only twenty-one – was already a senior Civil Servant. She and I immediately connected, and later we became best friends. A few weeks after the party she told me that she was renting a bedsit in Putney and was struggling somewhat with the rent. Would I like to move in with her? Although we had only known one another a short time, I was convinced that we would become the best of flatmates, and so I readily agreed. I had already started to worry about the daily journey between Queensway and our home in Kingston and life at home had become increasingly stressful and unhappy. All of these considerations made this big step an easy one to take.

Valerie, Brian, Graham and I became inseparable. I loved being in their company especially since Valerie had dedicated herself to helping me with my English. I had been attending evening classes at *Tiffins Girls School* in Kingston to improve my language skill but getting back there regularly was proving troublesome. This made Valerie's help invaluable. Sunday lunch at the Fedder home was quite an occasion, and both Valerie and Brian were always there. To my absolute delight, I was now included as Graham's girlfriend and, from then on, was treated as one of the family.

*

London! What an incredible shock for this young immigrant. We had learned a little about this World-Renowned City at school in Iran, but nothing prepared me for the pace, confidence and good humour of Londoners. Valerie was helping me with spoken English, but I still struggled to find some words. I also found the London accent a real challenge but was nevertheless completely thrilled with this new adventure that lay before me.

New Year's Day 1963 was my first ever day at work as an actual 'employee'; a day which saw some of the worst snowstorms Britain had experienced in 50 years. It took me two hours to get from Kingston to Bayswater, but I was *not late.* I was given a starched white coat and was immediately seized upon by an aggressive German member of staff called Ingrid. She gave me a duster and told me to do nothing but clean every item behind the counter. She was a merciless bully, and I was close to tears by lunchtime. Little did I realise however that matters were to improve considerably that afternoon.

At four o'clock a delivery boy came in with a magnificent bouquet of red roses, and I remember thinking how lucky someone must be to receive them. I was stunned when he asked if 'Miss Benjamin' was in the shop and I stepped forward to take them. They were from Graham Fedder wishing me a happy first day. I was tearful with joy but also thrilled that Ingrid, upon hearing the name of my admirer, immediately began to treat me with great deference. Graham was waiting for me when the shop closed and took me to dinner.

Meanwhile, my work at the shop was beginning to be noticed, and I was put in charge of the cosmetic counter. It was confirmed to me that sales had risen fifty per cent from this section alone, and my excitement was greatly enhanced by the murderous looks that Ingrid would frequently send my way. It was not long, however, before a nasty incident occurred which all but ended my brief career as a shop assistant.

Mr Fedder had a partner called Mr Green. He would often visit the Queensway premises and parade around in a very arrogant manner. On one particular visit, he was showing off to a lady customer. I was at the top of a wall-ladder replacing cosmetics on a high shelf when he loudly ordered me to get down. I was somewhat flustered and hastily tried to empty my arms and do his bidding. He was not prepared to wait ten seconds however and loudly told me to "come down at once"! I was overcome with the severity of his tone. Except for Mum and Dad, I had never had an adult shout at me before, and I was devastated. I always did what I was asked without comment, but the fact that he was using me to show off to some woman was too much to bear. I quietly descended the ladder, placed my arm full of stock on the counter, went to the back of the store and clocked out. Putting on my coat, I began to leave with him demanding to know where I thought I was going. Plucking up all my courage I told him I was leaving the shop and would not be returning.

Later that evening a very contrite Mr Fedder telephoned and explained that he had received an explanation from the store manager and would I please return the next day. He promised that Mr Green would never again engage with me in this way during his visits. I did not immediately agree since I was greatly shocked to realise that so-called 'bosses' could speak to obedient staff in this way. I was not yet eighteen, but this was a seminal moment in my life story. I resolved that as soon as was humanly possible, I would have my own business and that never again would I 'work' for a boss. The following day I told a very relieved Mr Fedder that I would go back to the shop.

I was not very tall and of slight build and this prompted some of the staff in the shop to refer to me as 'half-pint' or 'titch.' At first, I was upset by this, but it took the shop manager to explain that in England people most often only teased you if they liked you. I was soon a fully accepted and enthusiastic member of the team.

In the early sixties, contraceptives were still a subject that was broached with some difficulty, and this led to an achingly embarrassing episode for me. A young man came to the shop and leaned towards me whispering that he wanted to purchase some *French Letters*. This was a phrase that I had never heard in my life, and even if I had, I would not possibly have known what it meant. In my confusion, and hampered with my limited English, I thought he had asked not for 'French Letters' but for '**fresh liver**'! In my best English, I explained that he could buy this at the butcher's shop at the end of Queensway. He fled, and I retreated to the Managers office covered in confusion. Dear Mr Bristow – for that was the Manager's name – gently explained what a French Letter was AND what it was used for. Was a learning curve ever as steep for an innocent teenager?

My husband - of whom much more later- always maintained that something within their culture enables Assyrians to be perceptive to the skills of trading. I can only say that my arrival at Mr Fedder's shop ignited a passion for retailing that lives with me to this day. I realised how vital correct product display was to sales' volumes. I quickly learned how a friendly helpful persona achieved increased sales and above all, I learned the importance of profit as the engine that sustained business. When both *Christine Keeler* and *Mandy Rice-Davis* (of Profumo scandal fame) visited the shop with a lot of cash in their handbags, they always waited for me to serve them as I seemed able to accommodate their free-spending requirements. Needless to say, I had no knowledge at that time of their international notoriety but, my goodness, they spent a lot of money.

One could believe that my life was exciting and fulfilled. After all, I was successfully making my way in England without any support at all from my parents. Deep down, however, I was filled with uncertainty and doubt. I felt alone and vulnerable and frequently concerned about my future. More worryingly, I began to feel very unwell and soon found myself sitting in front of a very compassionate Doctor in Kingston.

I was truly impressed with his thoughtful understanding of my symptoms and, for the first time ever, I learned about depression. He assured me that my condition was mild and almost certainly temporary and prescribed a minimum dose anti-depressant that I was to take for sixty days. Within a week or so my symptoms began to recede, and I felt altogether more relaxed and energetic, but the doubts and insecurities I felt were ever present after that.

My time within the Fedder family was very satisfying and contrasted strongly with the miserable atmosphere at home with Mum. As is the custom with Assyrians, I had an obligation to look after my Mother, but it became clear that she intended to live off me as every one of her bills (utilities, telephone rates, etc.) were sent for me to pay. There were some months when I could hardly manage to cover all the outgoings so no wonder then that I spent a good deal of time with Graham's family. Mrs Fedder was a delightful and warm supporter of me and my development, and this led to a genuinely life-changing turn of events.

It all happened on a Sunday evening as the whole family sat watching the TV programme *That Was the Week That Was.* Towards the end of the show, an English belly dancer filled a small slot before the credits ran. I commented that I was able to dance like that. Everyone laughed good-naturedly but Mrs Fedder, full of fun as always, challenged me to apply to dance where this lady was currently appearing. If I were accepted, then she would pay for all the costs of a professional dance costume. The credits revealed that this dancer currently appeared at the U.K.'s first-ever classic Persian restaurant. With lots of jokes and laughter, I left them to return home.

The next day I plucked up the courage to telephone the internationally famous *Omar Khayyam* Persian restaurant in Old Street, City of London. I explained to the Manager that I was a Persian Belly Dancer, and he was immediately interested. He stunned me with his enthusiasm by promptly asking when I could come in for an interview. This I did the following day when I was introduced to a most accomplished quartet of musicians. I did a little dance for them, in a very modest twin-set with a sensible skirt. This was deliberate since, even then, I wished it to be understood that I had other means of earning a living and was not 'desperate' for this assignment. They were delighted with my small performance and implored me to start at once. I explained that I would need two weeks to make costumes and would then be able to start. In the meantime, the leader of the musicians said he would arrange a musical sequence to accompany my act. Back I went to Mrs Fedder, who was nothing short of ecstatic that I had had the nerve to apply. She readily paid for beautiful fabric and sequins, and I set about making a really stunning set of costumes for myself. And so, it was, two weeks later, I made my first ever professional dance debut.

All this time, Graham and I became virtually inseparable – much to the delight of his Mother and Father- and I was beginning to develop strong feelings for him. Our relationship, however, was clearly not one that would survive since it ended *dramatically* after a visit to the cinema in The West End. Graham had recently passed his driving test, and his parents had bought him a powerful

Lotus Cortina sports saloon car.   He proudly collected me from my flat, and we drove to the cinema.

He was incredibly reckless with his driving, but I tried to ignore this putting it down to lack of experience. While taking me home, however, he drove down Kensington High Road at very considerable speed and attempted to overtake a bus which *WAS ITSELF OVERTAKING* a family saloon. I screamed, and there was a shriek of brakes as our car skidded first left then right and finally shuddered to a halt. We both were shaken to the core and knew we had been inches from death or, at least, severe injury. I exploded with anger and swore that I would never again get into a car that he was driving. As if this near-death experience was not enough, he petulantly refused to accept that his juvenile behaviour was responsible for an incident that had diners running from restaurants to marvel at the spectacle.   The rest of the journey took place in total silence, and his solemn goodbye at my front door confirmed the realisation that our futures, after that, were destined for separate paths.

5

Many lessons learned

963 – I was now eighteen and was enjoying sharing a flat with Valerie in Putney. Life could hardly have been more exciting. My spoken English had improved considerably, and my hard work at the shop was being recognised. Also, I was about to commence a career *as a dancer.*

Ever since my teenage introduction to dancing at the hands of the redoubtable Madam Lilly I had retained a love of expressing myself through the intricate movements of Arabian Dance. To be given an opportunity to do this professionally was quite extraordinary.

Notwithstanding the excitement I was feeling, I was plagued with secret fears. I felt very insecure and was afraid that my good fortune could end tomorrow. I had no real support and suddenly felt alone and vulnerable. Such feelings never really left me, and I would have given anything for a sensible, loving Mother to give moral support to my endeavours. I simply had no reference point against which I could measure the break-neck speed of events.

Au Pair, dressmaker, Chemist shop assistant, belly dancer: where would this whirlwind of the past two years take me. All I knew was the deep-down fear that frequently frustrated my attempts at sleep.

My first performance at The *Omar Khayyam* was very well received by the diners, and I went back to the dressing room to calm my nerves await my final dance for the evening some ninety minutes later. Three other dancers performed that night, and I was surprised to see them hastily get out of their costumes and don evening wear. To my astonishment, they then went out into the restaurant to sit with diners. The Owner came to see me and asked why I was not joining them. I explained that I did not drink and besides I would not wish to chat with strangers.

The second night went very well save that, once more, he asked me to join the other girls sitting with customers. I insisted that this was something I was not prepared to do, and he left. The next night he came to the dressing room once more and addressed me in a surprisingly harsh voice explaining that such activity was 'part of the deal.' I was to sit with a customer and order a bottle of champagne. Each time this was done, I would be paid £1.00. Although I was very nervous in the face of this intimidation, I was able to tell him that, if that was the case then I had just performed my last ever dance at his restaurant. He swore and shouted that he would not pay me for the nights I had danced. He told me how stupid I was and that I should realise that no one else in England was hiring belly dancers and that I would never get any more work.

Outside, waiting for a taxi, I had time to collect my thoughts. The pay at Omar Khayyam was to have been £30.00 per week whereas I was earning £7.50 in the shop. I had paid the quartet £15.00 for the music, and Mrs Fedder had paid £18.00 for costume fabric. Also, I had paid for taxis to and from the restaurant for three nights. I could see that this was a somewhat painful and expensive introduction to the seedier side of London nightlife. My over-arching emotion, however, was one of *anger*. How dare this Maltese bully tell me that I would never dance again?

Two days later I bought a copy of London's *'What's on in Town'* newspaper and, armed with a pile of pennies, began phoning every nightclub or restaurant in the alphabetical list. To those that answered, I explained that I had just finished a contract at the Omar Khayyam and was free to accept more work. Refusal after refusal made this one of the most frustrating tasks I had ever undertaken. However, when I got to 'Y' on the list, I spoke to Mr Yung, the owner of *Yung's Chinese restaurant*. After a brief explanation of my situation, I asked him to understand that, were he to employ me, I NEVER would join any customers for drinks.

He welcomed this condition explaining that the Omar Khayyam had a very unsavoury reputation whereas he ran a 'family-friendly,' busy restaurant. We met the following evening and this dear, avuncular man, quickly introduced me to his wife and children. What followed was a three-month dance contract in the happiest environment I could ever have imagined. Whenever I was there, I ate with the family and was treated by Mr Yung as one of his children. Business increased significantly when word of my dancing spread and I was as happy as I had ever been since arriving in England. Apart from the pay of £30.00 per week I was also schooled in the intricacies of Chinese Food, which has led to a lifetime of pleasure with Asian cuisine.   This sudden 'wealth' made it possible to find a flat in Shepherds Bush; much more convenient for both the shop and Mr Yung's restaurant. It also meant that Bella could move in with me and share the rent. Although I was sorry to leave Valerie's apartment, she fully understood the reason, and we remained firm friends.

The restaurant had facilities on three floors.   The basement was set up for banquets and private functions while the ground floor was for the provision of quicker meals popular with pre-and post theatregoers. The top floor was designed for a more leisurely and expensive meal in something resembling a club atmosphere.   It was here that I did my dancing.

About a month after I started performing at Mr Yung's I was to benefit from a piece of luck which literally altered the course of my life. Before my usual evening routine, Mr Yung's daughter Mae told me that a private dinner party in the basement restaurant had expressed a wish to come up to the top floor to watch me dance. I was excited by this as it meant I would probably be dancing in front of eighty or so people. My dance was very well received and, as always, I retreated to my dressing room in the basement. A little later, Mae came into my room to say that a reporter had been in the audience and would like to talk to me.   I

55

was completely naïve about such matters but, out of politeness, readily agreed.

The reporter was Karen Meyer the Women's Page Editor of the London Evening News. She quickly put me at ease by explaining that she was one of the private dinner guests and that the occasion had been a retirement party for the Editor of her paper. A staff photographer had also been present and had taken some photos of me dancing.   Mr Yung, who was very proud of his young protégé, had earlier told this reporter that I was holding down a 'day job' as well dancing, and this had very much piqued her interest. Could she come to the shop the following day and photograph me at work?   I agreed, and she duly arrived with a staff photographer and took photos of me in my crisp white buttoned up uniform.

The following day started quite typically with me behind the counter in the shop when phone calls began to come from friends asking if I had seen the article about me in the paper. I got permission to go out and buy a copy and was completely staggered to see that I occupied a quarter page in the Ladies Section of the London Evening News with both photos and a flattering write-up. When I went home after work, I was aghast to see four photographers outside my flat! They were from National Newspapers, and all wanted to photograph the 'belly dancer.'

This memoir is a perfect opportunity for me to acknowledge Karen Meyer and the extraordinary boost she gave my fledgeling career, as she single-handedly introduced me to a wider public.   The article she wrote, along with several follow-up pieces, created a wave of publicity beyond my wildest dreams.

Life now took a surreal turn, and I was hopelessly unprepared for the head-spinning events of the following few days. I was still a somewhat unworldly girl from a village in Iran, and although I was learning fast, I lacked the experience to fully embrace the speed of events. Most noticeably, the restaurant was packed each evening, and professional agents were among the diners. Each of them left details of the work they could get me and the care that they would take to develop my career (!) First among these agents was the legendary bandleader Roy Fox, quietly confident that I would prosper under his stewardship. He was closely followed by a large agency called *Oriental Casting* whose reach in the UK casting environment was very extensive.

Roy Fox was an utterly decent man who convinced me that theatrical agents were, for the most part, cynically interested in their income and greatly less concerned for the healthy development of their clients' careers. He proposed that he use his considerable reputation to shield me from the worst excesses of the agents and offered to interview any who expressed an interest in representing me. The fee for providing this protective shield would be ten per cent of my earnings, and I happily agreed. He also explained the importance of a performer's name. My name at that time was Claire Sonya Benjamin, and he assured me that 'Claire' was not an appropriate name for an exotic Eastern dancer. 'Sonya' however, was perfect, and so it was that I became *Sonya* for all future engagements.

To my astonishment, Roy quickly secured a part for me in one episode of an ATV television series called *Crane.* The particular story was supposedly set in Morocco where I was to play a belly dancer. My nervous anticipation of the first time I would appear on film was rudely tempered when ATV was informed that, as I was not a member of the Actors Union *Equity,* then I could not appear. As it was not possible to join Equity unless you had a fully authenticated job as an actor; the outlook for me was bleak indeed. This was a classic *'catch-twenty-two' scenario* where one had to have been an actor before an Equity card could be granted but *could not act* without first having this card.

Roy Fox to the rescue! He persuaded ATV to write to *Equity* stating that no other person could play the *unique* role written into the script, and only this newly discovered *actress* Sonya could play the part. Within three days, I had my Equity card, and I proudly remained a member throughout the remainder of my performing career.

My spoken English was far from fluent at this time, and I was terrified that I would be asked to speak. However, the filming went off without a hitch, and I was extremely proud when the Director commented to the floor staff that he wished every actor was as co-operative and precise as I had been. The leading part in *Crane* was played by Patrick Allen, and I will always remember the kindness and support he showed to me in this my first ever TV role.

The following few months were a whirl of engagements. I was suddenly in demand to appear at functions such as celebrity birthday celebrations and private house parties of the wealthy. Fulfilling these contracts involved a good deal of travelling, and it became quickly apparent that I would have to give up my job as a chemist shop assistant. Mr Fedder was not at all pleased and, for the first time I saw how resentful he was that I had quickly established an independent career.

I had always seen dancing as a 'temporary' event in my life and that my core ambition was, and always remained, to save enough money so that I could have my own business. I had succeeded as a dressmaker and had impressed with my work in a chemist shop. It seemed to me that one of these skills would, at the appropriate time, assist me to achieve the real goal of being my own boss.

Some nights I was retained to do shows at two different establishments, and thus, my Lloyds Bank savings book had shown regular and satisfying deposits, and for the first time ever I was beginning to think that I could be both financially stable and confident for the future.

I was spending quite a lot on taxis getting to and from engagements, many of them late at night. With the encouragement of dear Mr Yung, I visited a car dealership which he had recommended and purchased a beautiful Riley 1.5 litre car. It was maroon with a beige interior and walnut veneer fascia. Mr Yung stood as guarantor for me so that arranging hire purchase was not a problem. I have *never* been prouder. My own car and an eye-catching one at that. I am not at all embarrassed to confess that the first stop I made on my way home was to a local chemist where I bought a lipstick shade that exactly matched the colour of the car.

It gives me no pleasure to recall – although I should for the sake of accuracy – that Mum had started telling her few friends that I was now wealthy. She began to insist that I should be paying her, even more, each week.   By now, I was settling her energy, rates, and 'phone bills, as well as my own rent and overheads and, could see that I was in danger of working ever harder just to provide for my family.   Articles about me appeared in some National Newspapers, and Mum seemed to have read them all. She astonished me by announcing that *Cliff Richard* had bought his mother a mansion in the countryside, and she was upset that I was not making the same arrangement for her. Our next-door neighbour in Kingston told me that Mum had boasted how I was now a millionaire. These revelations, sad as they were, made me even more determined to be financially independent, and after that, I accepted every dancing engagement that Roy Fox and other Agents secured for me.

I *loved* my new car. The feeling of independence it gave me was worth every penny of the significant outlay for its purchase. The longest journey I had undertaken was from my Shepherds Bush flat to Kingston, but every time I overtook a London bus, I felt great satisfaction.   A few weeks after buying the car Mum telephoned to tell me that Dad had called her from Turkey saying he wished me to *drive to Brugge* in *Belgium* to pick him up from one of his *India Man* treks.

Up to this moment, I had seen very little of my Dad. He hardly ever seemed to be in England and the few times we met he seemed incapable of taking any interest in my life whatsoever. Clearly, he and my Mother had little regard for each other and were drifting ever further apart. Try as I might, I could not persuade him to express any genuine interest in my life. Nevertheless, here he was asking me for help, and I was determined to show him my capabilities.

I was quite shaken with the enormity of the suggestion, however. *Belgium.* How on earth was I to undertake such a daunting journey when the longest run I had ever done in my new car was seventeen miles? I was shocked and somewhat afraid, but also in a peculiar way, tremendously excited with the challenge. If my Dad thought I could make that journey, then I must be capable of it.

No time to lose. I had to contact the London office of the *India Man* Company to get the exact address in Belgium. I telephoned the AA who was incredibly helpful with every aspect of route planning – including booking the ferry - and finally, I booked a one-night stay in a Dover hotel. By now, I was brimming with anticipation and could not wait to get started.

Journey to Dover, uneventful; hotel room, adequate; getting on board the ferry, less onerous than I had feared; now for the channel crossing. I had parked below decks with all the other vehicles and was making my way up to the passenger lounge when I was approached by an officer enquiring if this was my first crossing. I believe he decided to speak to me since I must have seemed somewhat unusual; a teenager with quite a sporty new car. I admitted that this was my first time on a ferry and he asked if I would like to meet the Captain. How could I refuse such an offer?

The Captain was on the bridge with other officers and greeted me warmly. No sooner had the introductions been made than I was overcome with such a wave of nausea that I was certain I would be sick any moment. Recognising my distress, they shepherded me to an area adjacent to the Bridge where there were a couple of deck chairs. They made sure I was comfortable and covered me with a blanket.

The next thing I knew was an anguished cry over the ship's loudspeaker insisting that *"the owner of the red car 407EJJ remove it immediately since it is stopping other cars from leaving the ship."* I was horrified. The officers must have completely forgotten about me fast asleep outside the Bridge, and now I was causing chaos below decks. I arrived at my car to be confronted by angry crew members and irate car owners and, somewhat shamefaced, hastily drove onto the dockside.

The rest of the trip was uneventful. Dad admired my new car but expressed no interest in the extraordinary few months of my life since I had last seen him. I vividly recall the drive back to the Channel coast during which I yearned for him to acknowledge my recent achievements but I waited in vain. There is no pain as spiteful as that for a teenager whose prowess and success is entirely ignored by her parents.

*

Mid-1963. We've been in England for three years. Time for a review of the family.

Joseph my Brother: Still at school. I had the impression that he was reasonably happy, but his English language skills still seemed inadequate.

Bella my Sister: Established now in the hair salon, and increasingly protective towards me if the press or agents tried to intrude.

Dad: Away a lot still driving Paddy's 'India Man' treks. Away as often as possible would be my guess!

*Mum: Now firmly established in her "I am always ill – there is never enough money"- syndrome. She had intimately bonded with her new best friend **Bingo** and was forever asking me for more money to fund this new love in her life. "Why did my miserable husband bring us here? It is a disaster. I never wanted to come".   This oft-repeated mantra would have been funny if it was not so utterly disingenuous.*

6

It's not all Roses

Looking back, I suppose it was inevitable that I would have my first adult relationship at this time. I was receiving flattering attention from several (mostly single) men as the London Press continued to run stories about the *'Chemist shop assistant turned exotic dancer.'* I shall call him David as I have no wish for this memoir to embarrass anyone.

He owned a small retail business close to the shop where I worked and often came into chat and buy things I suspect he didn't always need. He paid me considerable attention, and soon we were planning a future together. David did not see the need for me to be dancing most evenings and I let the agents know that I would not be accepting more bookings. I also gave up my lovely rented apartment as, by then, I had moved in with him. With all of these decisions made and our engagement announced, life could hardly have been better.

One of David's friends was a doctor who invited us to a small dinner party at his home. I was excited and flattered to be so immediately accepted into his circle of friends.

Ever determined to show me off in the best possible light, David insisted that he would buy me a dress for the occasion. We searched just about every shop in Knightsbridge without success, an expedition made the more miserable as I was struggling with an unusually severe headache. I weighed just forty-four kilos at this time and finding a garment small enough was virtually impossible but, despite the crunching pains in my head we continued searching until we finally found a beige cashmere skirt and sweater which fitted me perfectly. The dinner was not until eight which gave me time to take some pills and rest since the unrelenting pain was now barely tolerable.

Throughout the dinner, I was stricken with worsening pain, and I was aware that my vision was also somewhat blurred. *Was this how a migraine felt?* I did my very best to contribute to the evening, but I could not rid myself of the relentless waves of pain. I am sure the other guests could see that I was unwell but were far too polite to say anything. Thankfully, the evening drew to a close, and I could look forward to getting into bed.

By now, David was aware that I was unwell and I leaned on him heavily as we got into his apartment. In the entrance hall, my legs finally gave way, and I collapsed unconscious on the floor. David got me on to the bed and telephone Doctor Bell. He lived close by and was with us within ten minutes. I am told his diagnosis took five seconds – 'she has Meningitis and we need to get her to the Isolation ward of the Royal Brompton Hospital immediately.'

Meningitis!! It had struck me suddenly and severely. Headaches and a fever that had me really convinced I was dying. An ambulance rushed me to the hospital, and I remember little else for the next four weeks. The skilled specialist who looked after me explained that it had been "an extremely close call" when I first arrived at the hospital.

The next few weeks were a blur. The pain of a lumbar puncture is one clear recollection and the misery of nights alone in a sterile but unfriendly environment was another. There was certainly no call button to alert night staff if one needed them and, such was my distress that I was reduced to calling out for help with barely any success. A few days into my stay I was apparently found on the floor next to my bed by the morning staff as I had not managed to raise any nurse during the night. David was outraged when he learned of this and immediately paid for a private nurse to sit by my bed from eight each night until eight the following morning. I cannot think of a kinder response to the utter misery of my illness.

After four weeks, the brilliant specialist who had monitored me every day told me I was now able to return home. He added that I was still very frail and should take plenty of time to regain full health. As David worked every day, he would not be able to care for me, and it was, therefore, logical for me to stay with Mum in Kingston. My recuperation in her spare bedroom lasted exactly *two days.* She was just impossible. She would rise early and clatter around the house. Play pointless and loud morning television; bang pots in the kitchen and literally beat her breasts about how unwell she was and how much she hated her husband. I had to escape this madness as I felt myself slipping back into a bleak depression.

David took me back to his flat and arranged a meeting with the splendid Doctor Bell who took the time to explain the depression which almost always followed such a serious illness. The psychology of recovery from such events was very subtle, and he suggested that I might like to buy a little dog as a companion. He ventured the opinion that such an acquisition could possibly be more efficacious than a course of pills. Fascinated by this novel idea I set about finding myself a puppy which was why I found myself in Streatham a few days later buying a gorgeous miniature Pekinese puppy. I christened the adorable little chap *Chin-Chin,* and he must have come from an illustrious litter since no less a person than *Elizabeth Taylor* had purchased his two brothers the previous week.

Despite the pleasure of my new companion I had to recover my strength. I needed to get away to somewhere quiet and peaceful. What better place could there be than the same Austrian village that had been our temporary home three years before. David organised a flight, and I was soon back with the affectionate staff who had welcomed us so warmly when we landed on them from Iran. It was an excellent decision since everyone looked after me perfectly and I had nothing to do but rest.

David phoned me most days while I was there and began to make me feel a little selfish that I was looking after my health rather than being with him in London. I am not sure he realised how gravely ill I had been but, after two recuperative weeks, I flew home feeling fit again to face the World.   David was not able to pick me up for some reason, so I took a taxi to his apartment.

He was not there, and I began to worry. My concern dramatically increased when his mother told me that he was 'away' and that she was not prepared to say anything more. A few more enquiries evinced the fact that he was in the South of France with a lady-friend and evidently had not expected me to return so quickly.   I was weak, suffering from predictable post- meningitis depression, and my exciting new life was beginning to crash about my ears. After a painful hour of crying and feeling sorry for myself, I suddenly found strength and an enormous resolve to show this pathetic man that my life would be perfectly okay without him.

There are significant milestones in all our lives and, for me, this was such a one. I was now more certain than ever, that I had to look after myself and that I could not rely on anyone else to care for me. Before the end of that day, I had contacted my circle of booking agents and told them I was back in business. I was technically homeless, but within two days I had found a flat in Kensington and Bella moved back in with me.   Thanks to the *Classified Ads* section of the *London Evening Standard* I also found a job as an assistant in a local chemist shop. I worked there for four months until, once again, I had a full calendar of dancing engagements.

David pursued me ardently for a couple of months and his behaviour – including bursting in on a private dinner party at the *Park Lane Hilton* – came uncomfortably close to what, today, would be classed as stalking. None of his entreaties touched me at all. I did not feel spiteful towards him, but fidelity was a non-negotiable component of the relationship we had forged together. To my young Assyrian mind, the disrespect he had shown me had injured my heart and forgiveness was out of the question.

*

An unusual booking was made for me to dance at the London University Ball. The prospect of which made me both excited and nervous. This was not a London club or upmarket restaurant, and I was full of trepidation about the reception I would receive. Also, this would be far and away the biggest live audience I had ever encountered. I was soon totally reassured. The student committee members that had hired me were both respectful and helpful. I was accorded every courtesy and given celebrity status. My performance was a great success and led directly to an approach from *Trinity College Cambridge.*

This was yet one more seminal moment in my dancing career for it convinced me that my performance was suitable for more discerning audiences and was not just 'club entertainment.' I was determined not to be just another Belly Dancer but that I could perform to a level that deserved critical acknowledgement. I must also stress that 'celebrity' did not sit well with me. I was still somewhat shy and would never wish for my work to be discussed when in the company of others. I was very proud of my achievements thus far in my life but was not at all interested in the publicity hype that seemed to go hand-in-hand with the success I was enjoying.

Even I, a recent immigrant, had heard of the legendary *May Ball*, and I immediately accepted the proposal that I should be their headline act. Two days later, however, Roy Fox asked me to attend a meeting in London with another student committee from *St. Catherine's College*, also from Cambridge. It quickly became apparent that they had learned of *Trinity's* success in retaining me and, without much preamble, made me a counter-proposal. They offered to DOUBLE my appearance fee if I would perform at their May Ball – due to be held one day before *Trinity* - and also renege on my agreement with their bitter rivals. It was not difficult for me to explain that I had to keep my word to Trinity but, for exactly the same fee, I would also appear at their Ball. They showed significant disappointment that their 'Belly Dancer coup' had failed but readily agreed to my compromise proposal.

St. Catherine's, however, were not done with their plans to upstage their May Ball rivals and set about creating a story that would ensure every available ticket was sold. They took a three-quarter length picture of me in full costume and had printed across my bare tummy *"appearing at the St. Catherine's May Ball."* They then presented the poster to the Dean seeking his permission to display it in and around the College. Not surprisingly, he denied them their wish as this was surely far too racy for such a conservative academic. The student committee *knew full well* that permission would be refused, and the story was immediately leaked to the National Press which, next day, ran prominent stories... **Dean bans Belly Dance poster!** On the day of my performance, an enthusiastic young Turkish member of the committee proudly told me that every single ticket had been sold in record time.

I arrived at St. Catherines early in the afternoon and was met by the same young Turkish student who asked, very courteously, if I would take tea in his room. I agreed and followed him making sure that I had my faithful sixty-five-year-old pianist Stanley by my side. While preparing for my performance I was told that this young student was the Son of a Senior Minister in the Turkish Government.

The evening was a great success for me, and I marvelled at the riot of colour and energy that these young people produced. The whole evening was an unparalleled experience, and I was secretly pleased that both Stanley and I – once more, suitably dressed – were invited to join the boisterous party that carried on late into the night.

The Minister's Son asked me several times to dance, and finally, I agreed. This was to be a memorable waltz since he begged me to believe that he had fallen madly in love. Furthermore, great wealth lay in store for me in Turkey if I would agree to marry him. He had no reason to think other than the fact that I was a fellow Muslim. Had he known he was dancing with an Assyrian *Christian* I am sure the conversation would have been entirely different. He was actually the same age as me, but I really felt that this was puppy love, and I took care to deflect his proposal by fibbing that I was promised to another. Once the dance was over, I quickly grabbed Stanley's arm, and we left for our hotel.

The following evening, I performed at the ultra-prestigious *Trinity May Ball* and, such was the reaction that I was asked to repeat my performance two hours later. This lavish, grand event was a revelation to me, and I was awestruck at the carefree abandon that several hundred undergraduates brought to the occasion. I will also be forever grateful to the student committee who ensured that my every need was accommodated. This evening was an emotional one for Stanley since he had graduated in music from this very same college forty years before. Once again, we were both invited to join the revelries, but since it was then four in the morning, we quietly slipped away and began the drive back to London.

As dawn broke, we came upon a brightly lit transport café which had just opened its doors. We were suddenly taken with the idea of a good English breakfast and drew into a gravel car park which was already becoming busy with heavy goods lorries and vans of all descriptions. We found a table and Stanley ordered our meal from a large chap in a white sleeveless vest who gave the impression he had just that minute got out of bed.

While eating our most satisfying meal, we became aware that most of the other customers were staring at us with undisguised curiosity. Stanley was resplendent in his dinner jacket from the earlier performance and me, although I had changed into slacks and a jumper, was still wearing full stage makeup. And here we were, in the wilds of Cambridgeshire, miles from anywhere. What an incredible contrast for me at least; four hours ago, dancing under stage lights in front of several hundred enthusiastic revellers and now sitting at a Formica table, mopping up the last of my egg and surrounded by twenty or so *knights of the road.*

*

A few days later, and after considerable press coverage of my Cambridge exploits, I received a telephone call which actually *terrified* me. The Iranian Embassy required that I attend a meeting the following day. The tone of the conversation made it entirely clear that any excuse or prevarication would not be acceptable. It is important to remember that one frequently heard disturbing stories of individuals being harshly treated for no apparent reason.

I hardly slept that night and felt distinctly unwell the next morning when I stood outside the Iranian Embassy on the edge of Kensington Gardens. Taking a very deep breath, I introduced myself to the front door staff and was assigned an unsmiling male escort who took me to a sparsely decorated room. My surroundings were distinctly unfriendly, and I was left to sit alone for at least twenty minutes. After what seemed an age a rather severe man in his early-forties came in and sat across the desk from me.

"Miss Benjamin, are you not ashamed to be dancing in public with much of your clothing removed? Do you feel that this is proper behaviour for a young Iranian girl? Do you not understand that your parents must feel humiliated by this decadent exhibitionism?"

I had always been aware that there was a particular form of address to such overbearing bureaucrats and this recollection informed my reply at this testing moment.

"Honourable Sir, I take your wise words most seriously and have given much thought to the points you raise today.

I am pleased to say that my dancing costume covers a great deal more of my body than does a bikini. Also, my parents are truly proud of their daughter who came to this Country aged fifteen and has managed to make a career for herself so that she can help to support them. Finally, I am sincerely proud of my *Iranian* heritage and would never do anything to bring shame to our great nation."

I saw that my reply, offered with fawning subservience, seemed to take him somewhat aback. He paused to read some notes from a bright green folder he had in front of him and then changed the tone of the interview completely.

"Well Miss Benjamin, your answers are satisfactory which allows me to say that I would like to invite you to join me for dinner at my club tomorrow evening. My driver will pick you up at, say, eight?"

I was *staggered.* This immaculately dressed, smooth-talking Embassy Officer was suggesting a *date.* A great relief swept over me, but I was still on my guard against the possibility of him losing face in front of a mere woman.

"Sir, you do me great honour with such a generous invitation, but I fear my Fiancé will very possibly misunderstand your kind offer and he is a man of considerable temper as I know to my cost."

This clearly ruffled his composure, and he hastily agreed that dinner was perhaps not a good idea. The meeting over, the same unsmiling acolyte took me to the front door where, with great relief, I re-joined the Twentieth-Century by treading the welcoming streets of London once more.

7

Much, much more in '64!

This year was becoming the busiest ever for me which was perfect since I was saving every penny I could towards the ultimate wish of owning my own business.

I was very excited to find myself acting opposite *Donald Sinden* and *Elizabeth Sellars* in one of ATV's *Play of the Week* series and, even more, surprised to appear in an episode of *Champions,* a hugely popular 1960s series in the sci-fi genre. All of this slotting into an increasingly hectic schedule of night-club appearances.

Sometime in the Spring, I was approached by a significant booking agency called *Party Planners* who had retained me to dance at the twenty-first birthday party of the Belgian Ambassador's daughter. The instructions were quite specific - I was to get to his Belgravia mansion and speak *only to his wife.* She welcomed me into a small study and explained the need for the subterfuge. They had announced to all the invited guests that they had had me flown over from Cairo as a speciality performer and that I spoke no English. This was my first excursion into the realm of private performances for notable celebrities, and it was therefore very easy for me to sign up to this minor deception.

The entrance hall to this spectacular home was a large gallery and from its tessellated floor twin staircases arched up to a first-floor picture gallery. Mid-way through the evening, it was arranged for my music to begin through a concealed speaker system. I was then to appear from a side room and just start to dance among the guests. I was not keen on this idea as I thought my much-practised routine would hardly survive a milling throng of party-goers but, on the basis that the customer is *nearly* always right, I agreed.

Come the time, it turned out to be a consummate success. Once I appeared, the visitors fell back to the gallery walls allowing me all the space I needed. Also, the twin staircases were immediately filled with people all looking down on my performance. I do not believe a top film director could have staged this scene better and I danced my heart out. I finished to rousing applause and some cheering and retired to my little private room. The beaming hostess joined me at once and was fulsome in her praise and thanks. Now, she wished me to accompany her to the party so that she could introduce me to some of her grander guests.

"Please remember Sonya, you speak no English."

Thus, I was wheeled around the room full of society guests and answered all their enthusiastic questions with "Tink yo sou mech. I very hippy Heah."

*

One event in 1964 was of overwhelming significance to me and dwarfed all the other exciting acting and dancing jobs I undertook. Once again, I was indebted to *Party Planners* who had negotiated for me to appear at one of the UK's premier social events. The memories of this high-profile engagement occupy a prominent seat at the high table of my career reflections. Allow me please to set the scene by reproducing the brief I received from the agents.

Date: Third Saturday in June 1964

Event: A summer ball to celebrate the end of *Royal Ascot Week*

Venue: The mansion called *Ascot Place* set in four-Hundred acres in North Ascot

Guests: Five hundred of the 'great and good' of London Society

Hosts: H. J. Heinz the second, President of the World-famous Heinz food empire

Star Attraction: Joe Loss and his orchestra plus me!!!

My contract always stated the fee plus 'first-class travel expenses.' Because of this, the remarkable Mrs Heinz sent her personal Rolls Royce and chauffeur to collect me from my Kensington flat. My head spun with the sheer opulence of this luxurious car and the relaxed journey down the A30 was the perfect start to a memorable occasion.

I just could not believe this was all happening. Barely three years ago, I was dumped in Kingston without a single word of English, and now, with heaps of good fortune and a lot of hard work, I was the headline entertainment at one of the most sought-after social events of the year. I arrived and was met by Mrs Heinz ("now, my dear, you really must make sure you enjoy your stay with us") She was a stunning lady who oozed elegance and, I was to learn later, an extraordinary person in her own right. Her kindness and consideration towards me were nothing short of perfect. She insisted that I saw everything there was to see and so before the festivities began, I was taken on a tour of the truly magnificent grounds which concluded besides a truly impressive lake.

The lake! It was a scene straight out of a nineteen-thirties Hollywood romance. There were, at least, twenty small rowing boats with couples in them. Each was lit by a Tiffany-style lantern and had a little table supporting champagne and glasses. It was perfect June evening weather, and I was enchanted by this most elegant scene of British society. I must have stayed watching this magical sight for too long as I was politely reminded by a member of staff that the time was approaching for my performance.

As I walked away, I heard a very muted call to the boats announcing that the entertainment would commence in thirty minutes.

I cannot remember being so excited ahead of a performance. The Joe Loss Orchestra was just about the biggest thing in big band dance music at the time. Such was the power of his name that he had a 'second' Joe Loss band that would play at functions without him. Tonight, however, was his premiere orchestra with him leading it throughout the entire ball. The power and ingenuity of his musicians made my music score sound worthy of a film epic, and I do not believe I had ever danced better than I did that evening.

It was very late of course when I finished and had changed, and my thoughts turned to home. Suddenly, however, the graceful Mrs Heinz was by my side stating in very emphatic tones that she could not possibly allow me to be taken back at such a late hour. Another of her personal assistants – 'How many did she have I wondered?' – showed me to the second floor where I was given a room that any Princess would have been thrilled to call her own.

The following morning, answering a quiet knock on my door, I saw a neatly arranged tray with toast, orange juice, and quite perfect English Breakfast Tea. I later found a set of rear stairs leading down towards a kitchen and met the chauffeur drinking coffee and waiting to take me back to the reality of my flat and the dress I was making for my sister Bella.

*

Two months after the Ascot event my agent was contacted by representatives of a major stockbroking family. Someone had seen my act at Ascot and was thinking of employing my services at a very ambitious house party in the North of England. Initially, however, would I agree to an informal chat with the gentleman arranging the event?

Ever cautious but intrigued I duly presented myself at the stunning Belgravia home of *Neville Blond* the Publisher. I was accorded exaggerated respect and was introduced to *Peter Henriques*, a well-known stockbroker. He explained that he was arranging a lavish party in his Chester home to celebrate his wife's birthday. The theme would be *The Arabian Nights,* and he was hoping that I would repeat my *Ascot* performance as the centrepiece of the evening.

It was evident to me that he was attaching enormous importance to this party and that our chat was his way of ensuring that I had the right personality for what he had in mind. His enthusiasm and clear commitment to the event was truly infectious, and I happily agreed to appear. First class rail tickets were provided for myself and my pianist, and we were invited to arrive a day before the event.

I will never forget our arrival. We were met on the platform by Mrs Henriques accompanied by her three adorable children. They welcomed me as though I was a member of their family and I vividly recall feeling extremely emotional at the unguarded warmth they all displayed.

Once at the house, Mrs Henriques explained that she had organised for us to have the use of the Butler's *Mini car* as she wished us to explore the Chester area. Before this, however, we were shown to an elegant dining room where an excellent lunch had been prepared just for us. We spent the rest of the day exploring the glorious countryside around this historic Roman city.

The day of the party was exciting indeed. Everyone was in costume appropriate to the theme of the evening, and Mrs Henriques dazzled in a *'Cleopatra'* style gown and headdress. A little before festivities began, Mr Henriques visited my room and asked if I felt able to do him a personal favour. Would I make up his wife's face *Cleopatra-style?* I happily agreed and was secretly very proud of my handiwork when she later swept into the party.

And what a party it was. The mansion had very extensive gardens into which had been built the largest marquee I had ever seen. Not just a marquee but a faithful representation of a great Bedouin tent. Expansive drapes, heaps of cushions, and rugs aplenty made this an incredibly realistic environment for such an *Arabian* party.

My performance was very warmly received and, once more, I was aware of the social standing of the guests as I immediately recognised The Duke and Duchess of Bedford paying close attention to my dance. Back in the small anteroom which was where I prepared for the performance, I made ready for a quiet retreat to my bedroom. This idea was thwarted, however, by the appearance of Mrs Henriques who was absolutely thrilled with the success of her *exotic Arabian dancer.* Such was her pleasure that she implored me to come and join the party. I explained that I had nothing to wear other than the casual outfit I had arrived in the day before.

"My dear Sonya. Come and have a peep into the marquee. Every lady is dressed as some sort of a belly dancer, and all of the men are resplendent in Arab dress. Do you have another belly dance costume?"

I owned up to the fact that I always brought two outfits to a performance in case of accidents and she persuaded me to change and join her with her friends.

I *always* had a rule that I would *never* be seen by my audience in costume after dancing. I always felt to do so would diminish the authenticity of the dance story that I had just created on stage. On this occasion, I just could not say no to this wonderfully warm lady and so, dressed in outfit number two, I accompanied her to the party. I am certainly glad that I did as it gave me an opportunity to meet many notable celebrities including Henrietta Tiarks – also known as The Duchess of Bedford – who was expensively dressed in her Arabian costume.

The next morning, a return train journey to the normality of London and more thought to how I could realise my dream of one day having my very own business.

The remainder of the year was very busy with dance engagements including several more house parties outside of London. Memorable amongst these was a visit to Leeds where I danced for the Senior Executive Team of De La Rue, the banknote printers along with the top team of their security ink supplier. The Chairman of the ink supplier had kindly offered for me to stay at his home that night and any instinctive reservations I had were dispelled when his wife insisted that I accept.

Their home was simply incredible. Two great cottages had been amalgamated into a single, imposing country home and I was completely stunned with the perfection of the furnishings. My bedroom had an ensuite bathroom of generous proportion, and I felt very privileged to be in such elegant company. This experience also taught me that one did not necessarily need to live in London to enjoy the best of life. I had now seen, first hand, how some very successful families enjoyed wonderfully fulfilled lives without the need to submerge themselves within the claustrophobia of London's Mayfair. And how lucky was I to have the chance to visit these regions of England and meet some generous and kind members of the social elite?

Time for a new career

My twentieth birthday was fast approaching and although I was busy with dancing engagements and the occasional spot on television I was not really satisfied with my life. I still remained a private person and, invariably, hurried back to my flat after a dancing engagement. I had a small circle of good friends and enjoyed eating out or seeing shows with them, but I completely avoided the temptation to join the social scene that beckoned as a consequence of the publicity I was receiving.

My thoughts continually turned to ways in which I could start my own business. Dancing was excellent and more than paid the bills but I always saw it as a temporary way of earning my living. I was sure that such a life could not successfully continue for many more years, and it was this realisation which helped crystallise my thoughts towards a change of career.

I needed to carefully assess what capabilities I possessed. I was now a successful dancer with an established reputation. My English had improved significantly and this, along with my fluency in both the Farsi and Assyrian languages, allowed me to offer myself as trilingual. Also - and thanks to Nana Luba's early mentoring - I had proved I could earn a living by dressmaking. Finally, I had demonstrated my ability in chemist/perfumery store retailing.

Armed with this personal audit and confident that a future in retailing would be my best way forward, I began to look for a shop that I could rent. I had decided it would either be a boutique dress shop in which I would hand-make bespoke garments to order, or a perfumery. After a couple of weeks of fruitless search, I finally found a small shop in Blandford Street, Marylebone. It was too small for my dress shop plan but ideally sized for a perfumery. My financial resources were limited, but I did have enough to pay the lease premium and the first quarter's rent.

By carefully observing Mr Fedder when I worked in his Queensway store, I knew that 'footfall' was the overarching priority to success in retailing. Thus, before committing to the lease, I parked my car at the end of Blandford Street for several hours and tried to assess how many people would walk through during an average day. I quickly observed that several sizeable groups of young women would pass the shop at regular intervals. I plucked up the courage to ask one of them who they were and was thrilled to learn that they were head office staff from the *Marks and Spencer* Headquarters in Baker Street. They had to pass along Blandford Street to get to their canteen in Manchester Street.

I could not believe my luck. A regular flow of young salaried women would pass by at least twice each day. Armed with this very positive information, I took the lease and set about the task of opening my first shop. Although I had experienced some memorable moments from my dancing career, this was even more exciting. I had finally achieved the dream that had lived with me since we first arrived in England – *I now had my own business.*

I had enough money to obtain the lease and to pay three months' rent in advance but was only able to fill the shelves with stock because I was known to the perfumery company representatives from my time working for Mr Fedder, and they agreed on credit terms for the initial deliveries. I was always aware that this small retail business would not keep me and that I would need to continue dancing. Worryingly, dancing engagements temporarily ceased, and It was clear that I was facing considerable short-term difficulties. Life had already taught me to have a 'plan B', and I was mentally prepared – if needed - to go office cleaning from, say, six until nine in the morning and then run the shop for the rest of the day. However, such a plan remained unexplored as good fortune was about to smile upon me once again.

9

A Navel Experience

The week the shop opened I was contacted by a Public Relations company who were not known to me. They asked if I was prepared to audition for an Israeli family who had come to England to set up a luxury restaurant. I was not in the habit of doing 'auditions'- if someone wished to hire me, then they could watch me dance at one of my engagements. Necessity, however, encouraged me to ignore my own rule, and I found myself in the suite of a luxury Mayfair hotel dancing in front of the whole family including children. They were very pleased indeed and immediately offered a three-month contract at a fee which would comfortably cover my overheads for an entire year.

The opening night of the *Tamarisk* Restaurant in South Kensington received considerable publicity and was attended by many TV celebrities. Once my performance was over, I was invited by the family to join the celebrations. They sat me at a table with Benny Hill,

Frankie Howard, and Dick Emery. I really did not know these famous comedians, but I was soon aching with laughter at their spontaneous wit. Subsequently, it was explained to me that they were famous for their bawdy humour, but they were very courteous towards me and made sure that I had all the food and drink that I wanted. For the next three months, I danced nightly in this middle-eastern style nightclub-restaurant.

The financial cushion provided by the *Tamarisk* contract gave me the opportunity to devote my energy to the shop, and soon *Sonya's Perfumery* was beginning to develop a regular clientele. I always enjoyed serving my customers and – if I had ever had any doubts before – I was now certain that retailing was fulfilling my ambitions most positively.

The PR company responsible for the *Tamarisk* contract was owned by Jack Lewis, an ex-Daily Mirror reporter. He had asked that I pose for publicity shots in connection with the restaurant opening, and I happily obliged. About a week later he telephoned me to ask if I had ever considered insuring my midriff since an operation scar would certainly put paid to my belly dancing career. Understandably, I was very surprised by his suggestion but also intrigued and told him I would give it some thought.

A few days later I contacted my Insurance Broker and put the proposal to him. He exploded with laughter telling me that he did not believe such a policy could be secured but that he would consult colleagues in his office. Later that day he called back to confirm that it wouldn't be possible to arrange such insurance.

I forgot all about this matter until a week later when my broker called again to say that there *was* one company that would consider arranging an insurance policy for my midriff and that company was the World Famous Naval insurance business *Lloyds of London.* The bad news, however, was that it would cost twenty-five pounds per year. In 1965, this not inconsiderable sum would have bought fully comprehensive insurance for the Mini car for a year, but I told him to carry on with the arrangements.

The press immediately grabbed onto the story of *"Naval insurer insures a navel."* Just about all the National newspapers ran the story, but the most surprising thing was that it was also carried by the international news agency *Reuters.* They obviously had a photo of me in their archives as it, accompanied by suitable text, literally went around the World, appearing in Australia, South America, and the USA.

Of all the column inches about this insurance, I thought the Evening Standard put it best. Their reporter finished his interview with me and asked what I would do later that evening. I told him that I was dancing at The *Tamarisk*. His article faithfully reported my comments but added that perhaps this dance venue should be pronounced *'tummy-risk.'*!

The press now began to become interested in *"The belly dancer who also owns a shop, "* and I was soon being interviewed and photographed in my Marylebone perfumery during the day. The reporters were quite insistent but never rude, and the publicity benefit for the shop was excellent. This unexpected and massive publicity boost gave me a choice of dancing engagements for the next two years.

During one such interview, I mentioned the inconvenience of living in the Olympia district when my new shop was in Marylebone. To my surprise, several people visited me in the next few days offering the chance to rent flats in the immediate area. One such visitor – I shall call her Jane – was a striking redhead in her mid-twenties who was later to tell me that her husband had recently died and she had benefitted from a substantial life insurance policy. She explained that she was renting a large flat two streets away from the shop and was looking for someone to share it with her.

Jane had an engaging personality and while viewing her apartment surprised me greatly by suggesting that she should buy a fifty-per cent interest in my shop so that we would become equal partners. I did not need to ask for time to consider this idea since I had no intention of ceding any of my hard-won business to another person particularly someone who had already let me know that she never needed to work again as she was financially secure. This unexpected offer subconsciously reinforced the determined belief – a belief that informed most of my business decisions after that – that I would always *be my own boss.* The humiliation I felt at being chided in Mr Fedder's Queensway shop when I had done nothing wrong would never leave me, and I celebrate each business day by having to answer to *no one* for my actions. I moved in with Jane, and we got on well together. She was an ardent soccer fan, and with the 1966 football World Cup coming, she implored me to share every TV moment with her. I was not a fan of football but was as ecstatic as she when we finally triumphed in the final.

*

This period of life in London reinforced the core belief that having my own business and not being dependent on a dancing career was correct in every respect. I Had good friends but was not close to anyone in particular. I still occasionally received determined offers from men who had seen me dance, but the Assyrian girl inside the exotic costume was now more cautious about any relationships initiated as a consequence of my dance routine.

Despite the impressive list of engagements stretching ahead, and the stability of *Sonya's Perfumery,* I felt very alone when it came to making important decisions. I did not have a mentor or a 'rock' to turn to in the face of adversity. There was no loving mate with whom I could share my concerns. I suppose one's parents would be the obvious choice in such situations, but I felt that I had been 'mothering' my Mum for the past seven years. I simply could not imagine ever asking her for advice. Dad was similarly disconnected from the reality of London life and stayed out of England as much as he could.

I was also painfully aware that I was – certainly as far as the shop was concerned - a woman in a Man's World. The bank manager who cheerfully suggested that my shop had failed when I asked for a short-term increase in my overdraft, typified the negativity that sometimes confronted me. I was determined to be independent and show that I could manage my own life, but there were often times I would have loved to have someone to whom

I could turn when important decisions presented themselves. I was only twenty-one and had not come from a worldly background, and the superficial success of dancing obscured my lack of experience in many areas.

This was amply demonstrated when I was invited to a very exclusive Grosvenor House cocktail party by the PR firm responsible for several of my dancing engagements. The evening went well, and I was soon in conversation with a middle-aged man. He stood very close and was mildly patronising with his questions about what I did for a living. I was somewhat disconcerted by his repeated questions, excused myself as soon as I could, and quietly got a taxi home. The next day a plainly irritated member of staff telephoned to say how annoyed *Henry Mancini* was that I had terminated our chat. I was *mortified*. This great musician was at the height of his fame, and of course, I knew him by reputation, but I had no idea what he looked like.

Six months later, I was criticised in similar circumstances for not paying more deference to the singer *Lou Rawls* but, once again, I had no idea that I was talking to such a celebrity.

I was happy dancing and enjoyed the enthusiasm my performances received but felt most fulfilled when in my very own shop. I put all my energy into *Sonya's Perfumery* and had the satisfaction of seeing an increasing number of regular customers. I bought stock cautiously and regularly refreshed the window display with fashion jewellery items purchased from a local wholesaler. I was aware that I had learned a great deal while working for Mr Fedder and this experience was invaluable during the early months.

A typical day would begin with me opening the shop at nine and closing around six. Then, quickly home to my apartment for a snack meal and a bath. I would drive myself to *The Tamarisk* where I would dance at nine and again at eleven. Between shows, I had a dressing room where I spent the time making or improving my costumes. Home at about 12.30 a.m., where I would bathe my feet for a half an hour while eating supper. Into bed a little after one O'clock and then up at seven for another day. Yes, it was tiring, but I was building my independence and the less I ever had to depend on others, the happier I would become.

*

Mid--1965. The Benjamin family have now been in England for five years.

Joseph has left school but stays at home with Mum. He seems to have no inclination to work

Bella is now married to an Australian called Eric and will emigrate to Australia before the end of the year

Dad. Busy as ever driving for India Man and contriving to spend as little time as possible at home in Kingston

Mum. Just the same but ever more demanding for money from me now that I am a "wealthy woman,"

10

1966, The World Cup and Pelé

My contract at the *Tamarisk* had now ended, and I was very pleased to accept a calendar of bookings at several of London's most famous nightclubs. I would say that the popularity of my performance was at its highest during this year as I made a succession of guest appearances at one famous venue after another. As busy as I was, there was still time to reflect on the brutal treatment I had received from the owner of the *Omar Khayyam* in 1963 and his parting words warning me that I would never get work in London unless it was with him. I just hoped he saw all of the publicity surrounding my current success!

For all the pleasure I derived from appearing at such prestigious venues as *The Blue Angel* and *The Embassy Club* it was, nevertheless, family matters that seemed to dominate my time. Mum was becoming increasingly troublesome and had taken to visiting me at my shop to ask for money out of the till to cover her debts. I was still paying all of her utility bills, and so I had to conclude that she was gambling with any money Dad gave her.

More and more, she would lament how desperate she was to have her Mother (Nana Luba) come to live with her in England and would I pay for her to come?   As I have previously explained, my love and gratitude to Nana Luba were boundless and the thought of spending time with her in London was very exciting. The idea of such a visit began to form in my mind.

I began to research the practicalities of arranging a trip to England and was shocked to learn that a passport plus an exit visa alone would be more than five hundred pounds and this along with the cost of the flight was well beyond my resources. By now I was wedded to the idea of having Nana Luba visit us and so set up a savings account. I began to accept additional dance bookings to get together enough money to bring her over but still needed a bank loan to finance the visit. It took a little over a year, but in the Autumn of 1966, I was able to collect my wonderful seventy-year-old Grandma from Heathrow for her first ever journey outside Iran.

The 1958 earthquake in Iran had destroyed my Grandparents' restaurant and seeing their years of hard work reduced to rubble had made Nana Luba quite ill. I always hoped that getting her to London would enable me to pay for medical treatment to assist her back to health but, meanwhile, I was terribly worried how she would cope with suitcases, travel documents, etc. for this, her first ever international journey.

I waited anxiously at Visitor Arrivals desperate to get a glimpse of her. After a short while, she appeared accompanied by two handsome young Iranians who were carrying her bags and chatting as if she was their *mother*. I thanked them profusely for their assistance, but they stressed how glad they were to help someone with such a sunny disposition. After a tearful reunion, the next stop was Kingston where Mum had prepared a typically over-generous Assyrian meal. I left them both busily catching up on all the news since our departure from Iran.

For once, Mum had got her wish and seemed truly happy to have her Mother with her. Imagine my surprise, then, when three weeks later Mum telephoned with a mixture of anger and tears to insist that I remove Nana Luba at once since she was driving Mum mad. The next day I drove to Kingston and collected Nana Luba and took her back with me to stay at my flat.

Having Nana stay with me provided the opportunity I had long cherished to have medical professionals review her health. Dear Doctor Bell immediately agreed and booked her into his clinic for a comprehensive set of tests. I was overjoyed when he told me that she was in relatively good health for someone her age. She had signs of age-related arthritis in her hips, and her blood sugar was somewhat high but not yet diabetes level. He prescribed a low-dose tablet for slight blood pressure but was, overall, very satisfied with the results.

Nana was wonderful while she was with me. She insisted on staying up each night to welcome me home after my dancing and always had a foot bath ready. After a few weeks, however, it became apparent that she was missing Grandpa very much, and I bought her ticket to get her back home to Teheran.

*

With this family drama behind me, it was time once more to focus on every dancing opportunity so that I could repay the loan, I had taken to finance Nana's visit, and an extended contract at The Embassy Club was just what I needed. This was an incredibly professional venue with highly trained management, and it was here that the most spectacular example of my naïveté occurred.

I had just completed the second performance one evening when the Club Manager came to see me and said that a very famous celebrity had watched me dance and wished to introduce himself. I made it a rule never to go into the club after a performance, but the Manager said that Pelé would like to meet me. Suitably dressed in a floor-length robe, I shook hands with this imposing figure, and ever the polite young lady said: "Hello Mr Pelé, what do you do?" My dear husband Alan still cringes when this story is told, but I had absolutely no idea that he was the World's most famous footballer and that this was the year of the World Cup in England. To his great credit, Pelé was totally amused and returned to his table to regale his colleagues with our chat.

*

By now I had shared a flat with Jane for about a year and while it worked well, and she proved to be a good friend, I began to yearn to be on my own. I would come back from a dancing engagement and Jane would always be up watching late-night television with a bottle of wine open. She wanted nothing more than to share a glass and have a good gossip about everything and nothing, whereas I wanted to just bathe my feet and climb into bed.

My frustration must have shown since I was berated one morning by a regular customer who ran a successful accountancy practice nearby. He wanted to know where my sunny disposition had gone? I began to explain only for him to interrupt by telling me that one of his clients had, *that very morning,* been bemoaning the fact that one of his tenants had disappeared owing both rent and utility bills. He suggested I go to see this man without delay and that he would telephone ahead with a personal introduction. Later that day I met with the landlord who said that if I would take over the contract for the night storage heaters, then I could move in at once with a renewable seven-year lease.

Wendover Court in Chiltern Street represented all of my dreams come true. This quiet, elegant street nestled immediately behind London's famous Baker Street and sat near to the legendary home of *Sherlock Holmes.* It was unfurnished but had three excellent bedrooms, and it was *mine alone.* This was a happy day indeed. I was exactly two minutes from the shop and a member of the impressive Marylebone neighbourhood and, for the first time since arriving in England five years ago, I did not have to share facilities with anyone. I now had the challenging but joyous task of furnishing my new home which gradually saw the introduction of carpeting instead of the hastily spread newspapers that first welcomed me to my new home.

II

"Stop, Stop, Stop!"

Courtesy of Roy Fox, I found myself on the way to EMI's recording studio in Manchester Square London ready to fulfil an unusual dancing assignment. I had been asked to attend at short notice prepared to dance with *The Hollies* pop group. It was Autumn 1966, and they were the leading group of the time, comprising five musicians known as *The Hollies*- so called to honour the legendary Buddy Holly. They were achieving great success both sides of The Atlantic and would become memorable for such chart successes as '*The Air That I Breath.*'

A year earlier the group had been in New York and had been taken to dinner by Maurice Levy, the renowned impresario. The dinner was accompanied by a Cabaret, which featured a sultry belly dancer whose sinuous moves and provocative gestures left this relatively inexperienced group of Manchester boys utterly beguiled. It seems that this vivid experience never left them to the extent that early the following year Allan Clarke and Tony Hicks wrote a song in celebration of this dancer called *Stop, Stop, Stop.*

I am sure I will be forgiven for quoting the opening few lines as they capture the story behind the song perfectly.

> *"See the girl with cymbals on her fingers*
>
> *Entering through the door*
>
> *Ruby glistening from her navel*
>
> *Shimmering around the floor."*

In June and August of 1966, they recorded this track at the EMI Studios, and their management team hit upon the idea of a belly dancer performing in front of them as they sang. Enter Sonya with her full costume and a significant fake Ruby.

When I arrived at the studio, the group were polite but distinctly distant. At this time, they were at the height of their International fame, and I think they found it a little unusual that a girl aged twenty-one was not clamouring for their attention.

The management team explained the format, and I got changed in an adjoining room. The recording track had been successfully completed a few weeks before which allowed the group to mime to the music track, as I danced in front of them. This we did three full times so that the editors had plenty of material with which to produce the film. I was told that this would be the first ever video promotion of a pop song and would be shown on the TV show *Top of the Pops* plus dance venues internationally.

I would like to say that the recordings went without a hitch but the adhesive used to attach the fake ruby to my navel was inadequate, and the over-large stone would repeatedly fall out. A discussion took place where it was suggested that the shoot continues without this adornment, but the Production Manager explained that the film could not then be shown in America unless my navel was, at all times, completely obscured. *One learns something new every day!*

12

Always read the contract

Another busy year beckoned. The Blandford Street shop had settled down nicely, and I was now able to leave it in the capable hands of a couple of friends if I needed to be elsewhere.   A busy dancing schedule lay ahead of me, and I was financially stable once again.

Sometime in August, I received an excited call from one of my agents, Gaston & André in Regent Street. Miss André herself made the call and told me that no less a person than *Lee Kuan Yew*, the Prime Minister of Singapore had been in England on Commonwealth business. While here, he had been entertained at The Blue Angel Club and had seen me dance. He had expressed a desire that I am flown to Singapore in September to appear at his forty-fifth birthday celebration. His representatives were anxious to begin the negotiations.

Events had moved quickly, and in recognition of the very long journey this would be for a single appearance, the hotel group hosting the party had started to think creatively. They proposed that I be offered a two-week contract to appear at their two leading Singapore hotels in addition to my performance for The Prime Minister. The travel arrangements were in the hands of British Overseas Airways whose offices were close to Miss André's firm.

This was such an enormous departure from anything that I had done before that I went to Miss André to discuss matters in more detail. On the way, I called in at the BOAC office, and they confirmed that a business class reservation had been made in my name, but they had no knowledge of a *return booking.* I now began to have serious concerns about this 'opportunity of a lifetime' and spent time with Miss A. looking at the contract. Everything seemed perfect: the dates of my appearances at both hotels, details of first class accommodation and confirmation of the grand birthday party celebrations that would involve me. Rather ominously, however, the return journey was defined as − *'The artist to be returned to the UK by any transport at the discretion of the management.'*

I had terrifying visions of white slave traders handing me on to one another around Asia and finally dumping me onto a tramp steamer home when I was of no further use. Common sense prevailed, and I decided to decline this seemingly brilliant chance to experience my first ever overseas engagement. I was passing up the biggest fee of my professional career, and I could not conceal my anger at Miss A. and her agency. In their rush to have me sign this contract, they had utterly failed to check the details of the agreement and could well have consigned me to an unpleasant and frightening situation. Up to this point, I had tended to accept that agents had my interests at heart − how wrong was I. At the risk of losing future bookings from her, I immediately severed my relationship with this well-known and influential agency.

*

No sooner had this affair been erased from the diary when another overseas opportunity presented itself. This time, it was Malta and thank goodness the arrangements in the contract were clear and unambiguous. I was to appear at the leading hotel in Sliema Bay for two weeks. First class flights and accommodation plus an impressive fee made this an exciting new experience for me.

The manager in the Agency offices reminded me that I did not need to take a passport for this trip since '*Malta was technically part of England and that English currency was used throughout the Island.*' Totally satisfied with this explanation I set off for the airport *sans* passport. From today's perspective, this must make me look foolish but, at that time, I readily believed what I was told. The airport staff were understanding and explained that they *would* allow me to board the flight without my passport but only if I signed a waiver indemnifying the airline from any responsibility should the Maltese refuse to let me into their Country.

Luckily, I was allowed through immigration, and as soon as I was in my hotel, I telephoned Joseph to send me my passport by express postage. What followed was a very busy yet enjoyable two weeks made memorable by the overwhelming courtesy and friendliness of those I met. My visit was shortly after Malta had become independent and Dom Mintoff, the previous Prime Minister, was still a significant political force. The current administration had begun flexing its anti-British muscles by flirting with Russia, and I had been warned about encountering possible resentment, but the reverse was true.

When it came time to return home, I arrived at the airport to be met by staff who explained that they were aware I had no passport and that special arrangements had been made for me. I immediately explained that I now *did* have my passport, but they waved it away and took me directly to passport control. The smiling team in the booth proudly announced that they knew who I was as they had all seen me dance at my last performance the night before. I will never forget the excitement of the airport staff and their wish for '*Sonya*' to sign any piece of paper they could find. I was taken immediately by a VIP route directly to the plane and felt so tall that it was a wonder I could squeeze through the aircraft door.

13

The 'secret' Dance Invitation

A call from one of my Agents said that I was booked to dance in Paris in two weeks' time and would I call to discuss the details. I remember being so excited at the thought of my first engagement outside of the UK since my trip to Malta. The contract details were fine except that the name of the organisation hiring me was to remain a secret. I visited the VIP Travel agency in Curzon Street and collected a *first class* return ticket to Paris. I was to book myself into a hotel called *George Cinq* and because I had never heard this name before I wrote it down on a piece of paper.

The flight to Paris was memorable – my first ever first-class seat – and I was soon outside the airport and climbing into a taxi. I had virtually no knowledge of the French language so passed my piece of paper to the driver who seemed somewhat surprised at my destination. Arriving at the hotel entrance, I was taken aback by the timely and solicitous way that my taxi door was opened, and my luggage spirited inside the imposing entrance.

This magnificent and famous hotel took my breath away. I had been fortunate to visit some of London's best hotels, but nothing matched the splendour and opulence of the scene that confronted me. I immediately sensed that this was no ordinary hotel as everywhere I looked seemed to speak of wealth and high living. I became aware of a concierge holding my bag and gently guiding me to the reception desk. An immaculately presented receptionist looked at my Persian passport and explained that they *were* expecting me and that my suite (!!!) was ready. As an afterthought, she added that my King – The Shah of Iran - *had stayed with them the previous week.*

Hearing this I became very nervous. What if this 'secret booking' did not take place? How could I possibly pay for accommodation here with the few francs I had and many years before credit cards had been invented? The receptionist sensed my unease and looked somewhat pensive when I asked her, to please tell me who it was that had booked me. She gave me a reassuring smile and said everything was in order, but the name on the booking had to remain private. She added that I should relax in my room and that I would be contacted.

The suite was about the size of my flat at home, and I spent a little while just absorbing the sheer luxury of the décor and fittings. After a while, I called reception to ask about food to be told that whatever I wished to eat could be brought to me, or I could dine in any of the several restaurants that were open. I decided to visit a brasserie and ate just a single sandwich because the prices were astronomical and I was still privately concerned that I could end up being charged for everything.

A long and comfortable afternoon gave way to evening, and I was, once again, having to quell my reservations when there was a knock at the door. An Arabic gentleman dressed in an immaculate western suit asked if he could enter and I welcomed him to my sitting room. He was a model of propriety and thanked me profusely for agreeing to visit Paris to dance for them. At eleven p.m. would I, please take the elevator to the fifth floor where he would personally receive me.

I spent the next three hours worrying about the dance itself. I never danced publicly without first visiting the dance area and estimating distances that were crucial for me to maximise the impact of my routine. Obviously, this was not going to be possible tonight. Precisely on time, I entered the elevator which was already occupied by two sombre Arabic men both sporting small but menacing machine guns. It did not take much imagination for me to work out that I was going to be dancing for a group of very senior Arabs.

As promised, the same smiling gentleman nodded a greeting to me as I got out of the lift and ushered me into a substantial salon. It was a dazzling sight. A long oblong table centred the room, and it was heaped with all the delicacies one could imagine. Fruits, shellfish, caviar and many foods that I could not even recognise, covered the entire length of the table. That was the initial impact: the second was the twenty or so impossibly elegant young ladies each of them dressed in a seemingly contrasting designer gown. Their hair arrangements were beautiful and a more refined group of women I had never seen.

They were chatting with one another and taking little bits of food from the table and welcomed me warmly as I went to join them. They were all French, but there was enough English spoken for me to learn that they were aware that 'Sonya' had come from London to dance this evening. I eagerly seized the opportunity to press them about the group that I would be entertaining and was astonished to learn that it was not to be a group at all, but rather *just one man*.

This gathering of elegant ladies fascinated me, and I asked if they had come from an agency? They quickly explained that they were all on the books of the most famous 'Madame' in the whole of France and that they were highly paid Escorts. I was keen to know where they were staying to be told that they all had rooms since the host had reserved *the whole of the fifth floor* for his visit.

After a little while, I was escorted to a private room along the corridor and asked to get into my costume and prepare myself for a call a little later. As we left the salon, the host – One of Saudi Arabia's most Senior Princes – was in the corridor ahead of me and I watched as an assistant helped him remove both his elaborate headdress and cloak, to reveal him dressed in an elegant western business suit. I later learned that he was in France on a State visit and chose to spend his nights in this way. I averted my eyes and hurried to my room.

I was rarely nervous when dancing as I had experienced most environments and audiences by now, but I was genuinely terrified at the thought of appearing in front of this Prince of a desert kingdom. Surely, he will have seen the best dancers in The World? Would he ridicule this Assyrian girl who mainly developed her dancing skills in Britain? I got into my costume, did my best to relax and waited for the call.

I heard nothing for the next hour, and the wait was beginning to play upon my nerves. My doubts and insecurities bubbled to the surface once more, and I wished at that moment to be back in London without the pressure and anxiety that my current situation was causing me. I suddenly felt so lonely and would have given anything at that moment to be able to call a loved one who would reassure me. I wrestled with increasing doubts and was close to panic when at one a.m. there was a knock on my door and, swallowing my fear, I made my way to the salon. My pre-recorded dance music began playing through a lavish sound system and, forcing my knees to behave themselves, I went through the door to start my performance.

The scene before me was truly memorable. The Prince sat on an enormous sofa, and the girls were draped around him looking even more beautiful. Behind him were several deferential Arabs plus, at least, two 'minders.' To my immense relief, The Prince paid smiling attention to my dance, and on a couple of occasions, he clapped with genuine pleasure. When it was over the room gave me resounding applause, led by The Prince himself. I was escorted back to my room to change and then back to my suite at about three-thirty.

My flight back to England was not until that afternoon as I wanted very much to see the shops in the *Champs-Elysee* before my return. I had a light lunch and returned to my room to pack, only to be met in the corridor by the same smiling gentleman from the day before. He needed to pass an urgent message to me and could I give permission for him to step into my room. Once the door was closed, he explained The Prince was "delighted" with my performance and had requested that I cancel my return trip and dance again for him that night.

I immediately thought they were trying to get two performances from me for the price of one, and so fibbed that I had to be back in London for a dancing engagement that evening. I am sure he sensed my reluctance to be exploited in such a way as he hastened to assure me that, not only would they pay for two performances, but they would also pay the fee I would have been earning that night in London. Also, they would handle all flight cancellations and return me to Heathrow the following day in a private jet at any time of my choosing.

Being born in The Middle East, I was aware that my first duty was to pass my thanks to The Prince for seeing merit in my unworthy efforts to entertain him. I added that it would be an honour for the rest of my life if he would allow me, once more, to dance before him. The relief of the poor chap sent to persuade me was palpable. I wonder what would have happened to him if I had sent him back with a curt refusal? Come to that, *I wonder what would have happened to me?*

As if this turn of events was not surprising enough he then further shocked me by placing a white envelope on the table saying The Prince thought I would like to spend some time shopping. Opening it as soon as he had left I found eight hundred Francs, equivalent to some seventy pounds at the time. This nearly equalled my fee for a single performance – *riches indeed.*

The second night proceeded much as the first, save that the girls around him seemed to be a new group. He was a delight to dance for as he regularly showed his appreciation of my efforts and, once again I fell into my bed at three a.m.   Leaving Paris in a private jet the following afternoon is something I will always remember.   The airport staff must have known whose guest I was as they seemed to show exaggerated attention to my every need.

The flight gave me time to remember the nervous panic I experienced before the first of my dances two nights before, as insecurities once more began to crowd my mind. What if dancing engagements ceased from now on? How would I manage on my own without income? Why did I feel so desperately lonely? With a considerable effort, I subdued the sense of rising panic and concentrated on enjoying the remainder of the homeward journey.

Nana Luba, I wish you had seen me? I danced before a real Prince!

14

Suddenly I was surrounded by soldiers

A nother busy year was in prospect, and the shop seemed to be progressing well. It gave me considerable satisfaction to see that increased sales always occurred after I had re-vamped my window display. I was learning fast and began to expand the range of products to accommodate people who saw my shop as a local *drugstore*. Plasters, embrocation and many other 'bathroom cabinet' items were always in demand.

Sometime in the Spring, I was alone in the shop when, to my considerable surprise, my bank Manager walked in. He explained that a part of his duties was to visit his business customers at least once a year, and he apologised for not having made an appointment. "Just in the area" was his somewhat lame explanation but I was immediately sure that he wanted a surprise visit to see how this Assyrian *girl* was coping with a real business.

We chatted about my progress, and the Gods were with me as a steady stream of Marks and Spencer staff kept the till buzzing throughout his somewhat awkward visit. He finally prepared to leave but declared that he would like to buy some perfume for his wife before he went. By now I carried a significant range of superior fragrances from most of the major Houses, but it took him only a few seconds to select Revlon's 'Charlie,' a reasonable fragrance but oh! *So cheap*.

A few months later I was confident enough to change banks and so, made an appointment to visit Barclays in Marylebone High Street. I was understandably nervous about introducing myself to the new manager as my account was overdrawn and had hitherto been guaranteed by the avuncular and supportive Mr Yung. Part of the reason I wanted to change banks was so that I could release this father-like gentleman from the obligation of being my guarantor. I explained these facts to the Manager who immediately reassured me by saying that no guarantee would be required and that the bank would be very pleased to take on my account.

" You are the only person that has ever made a success of that shop, Miss Benjamin and I personally admire the bright and welcoming business you have built there."

I will *never* forget the overwhelming pride I felt at that moment. Here was a finance professional acknowledging the success of all my hard work in the past year. I believe he saw the impact of his words as I fought to hold back tears of gratitude and hastened to add he wished more young women could establish themselves in the way I had. At last, a recognition that I was a young *businesswoman* and not just a speciality dancer. I relished the association with this Manager, who believed in my business and supported me constructively for the next ten years.

*

At about this time I received another call from the excellent *'Party Planners'* company.

Would I accept a booking to dance at the Annual Ball of one of the British Army's most famous Regiments, *The Blues and Royals.* I believed them to be a part of The Household Cavalry, who were based in Windsor. First, though, would I attend a 'pre-event discussion' with a Captain from the Regiment.

The following morning saw me ringing the bell of an imposing townhouse in the very best part of Kensington and being invited in by a tall and relaxed young man perfectly attired in tailored blazer and cavalry twill trousers. He explained that he was responsible for planning the ball and had to be sure that my dance was 'appropriate' for this prestigious event. We discussed the many differences between classical Arabian belly dancing and some of the more commercial imitations that were wholly designed to titillate patrons in certain downmarket venues.

He appeared satisfied and asked that he be sent a copy of my music as the Blues and Royals orchestra would be playing throughout the evening. In turn, I explained to him that I would need to visit the venue several hours before the event to determine the floor area that my dance required. Everything was agreed, and I eagerly looked forward to my first ever visit to Windsor.

On the appointed day I was met by the same officer, this time wonderfully attired in his military uniform, and we made our way to the ballroom. The area was a hive of activity, and there seemed to be Guardsmen everywhere. I suddenly felt tiny being surrounded by guardsmen, each of whom appears to be at least a foot taller than my five feet two inches.

The Captain and I were alone in the centre of the room for just a moment when he leaned towards me and murmured "you do realise Miss Sonya that, before today, I have *never* met you." I was taken aback by this unexpected interjection but quickly imagined him, accompanied by his young wife, seeing my dance later that evening and failing to mention an interview in his home two weeks before. Sign of a guilty conscience I wondered?

As luck would have it the orchestra was rehearsing for the evening ahead, and I was pleased to introduce myself to the Conductor – or should I call him Bandmaster – who satisfied me immediately that he understood the nuances of my music score. *Particularly*, the sixteen-bar introduction to my dance routine.

Having assured myself that I had the floor plan in my mind, and having met such a professional musician, I was shown to my room to prepare for the evening.

At about half-past ten I was called and made my way to the entrance doors of a very crowded and somewhat noisy ballroom. *Catastrophe*! The orchestra leader, having noticed me at the door, abandoned the vital sixteen bar introduction and went straight into my dance music. This was a *disaster*. At the risk of sounding like a prima Donna –

something I assuredly was not – I just could not begin dancing from the doorway. A panicky young officer who had collected me begged me to just go in and start. I refused and told him to go to the orchestra and have them start again.

Recognising that he would not win the argument, he dashed to the stage with my message. After a little delay, my introductory music began, and I danced my heart out. The swelling notes of an excellent orchestra filled the room and gave me a surge of self-belief that I have never forgotten. I honestly believe the two-hundred or so diners sensed the almost magical intensity of my performance because they called me back into the room *three* times to acknowledge their appreciation of my efforts.

A nineteen-year-old Prince Charles was there that evening, but I certainly did not pick him out from the swirl of faces of that warm and enthusiastic audience.

*

Shortly after this never to be forgotten evening, an Agent contacted me with news of a two-week booking in Birmingham. Bella had a two-weeks annual leave without any plans as to how she would spend it so it was decided we would both drive there and make a holiday of our time together. Silly as it sounds, such a drive would be something of an adventure for us, and Bella asked the AA to give us a journey plan.

This was to be a pleasant contrast to the routine of London bookings, and I was looking forward to spending quality time with Bella.   We set off early and found our way Birmingham. The ring-road system was somewhat daunting but, as we were early, we did not head for our pre-booked hotel but decided to take a look at the club in which I was to appear. We finally found the venue not far from New Street railway station and parked the car nearby.

Bella saw it first and squawked with alarm. Several posters behind glass screens shouted loud and clear that this was a *strip club* and not a very prestigious one at that. How could the booking agent have been so stupid? As shocked as we were, we decided to go in and ask some questions.

We soon found the Manager, complete with a 'Brummie' accent that made him almost incomprehensible to our Assyrian ears.   My head was spinning, and I needed to find an excuse to get away. The music set up was on the stage, and I could not see a drum. I blurted out that a drum was vital to my act, and as there was not one then I could not perform. "No problem," he said, "I'll have one here this evening."

 "my act does not include the removal of any clothing" was all I could think to say to which he countered that appearing at his club would make me a star so I should really be grateful for the opportunity.

While this truly awkward conversation was stuttering on Bella had removed herself a respectful distance away and had begun to play a slot machine. As I finally gathered my courage to say I was not prepared to appear, I heard a bountiful jingle of coins. Bella had *won the jackpot.* Consumed with embarrassment, we both fled back to the car where Bella found that she had won five pounds. The petrol for our return trip to Birmingham was one pound, so at least we were not out of pocket, and Bella had earned more than a week's wages from her slot-machine flutter. We were angry and miserable in equal measure, and the return journey was a study in sadness and frustration.

On reflection, I suppose such incidents are a predictable hazard to a young professional dancer. I could not really blame the Agent on this occasion. They must have been dealing with many clients at the time, and this seemingly lucrative booking was just nodded through. If nothing else, it gave me many hours while driving to catch up on loads of stuff with my sister.

15

An Unwelcome Invitation

It was a casual suggestion from two of my friends that led me to an alarming and somewhat sinister confrontation.

We had just finished a light supper at one of the Regent Canal boat restaurants when it was suggested that we 'go on' for a drink at a friend's house in Albany Street just on the Eastern boundary of Regents Park.

I readily agreed and set off to walk the short distance. On the way, my friend explained that *Elizabeth Sellars* and *Mary Scott-Hardwicke* - both established film actresses - lived in the house and there was always an open invitation. I was very interested in meeting *Elizabeth Sellars* again and wondered if she would remember that we appeared together in an ITV *Play of the Week* a couple of years before.

The house – and what an imposing detached building it was - had belonged to Sir Cecil Hardwicke, the highly successful British actor who found fame in Hollywood where he made many feature films from the twenties to the fifties. Mary was his second wife whom he married in 1950. They divorced in 1961, and he died not long after this.

We were welcomed warmly, and drinks were poured while we made ourselves comfortable around an over-sized mahogany coffee table. Sometime later, an Indian gentleman entered the room and, after polite introductions, took a vacant seat next to me. I would estimate him to be sixty years old, and he was perfectly attired in an expensive and elegant lounge suit. While he was consistently polite, he had a somewhat patronising air towards Elizabeth and Mary which left me feeling a little uncomfortable. As it was now approaching midnight, I suggested that it was time for me to make my way home and we made ready to go.

This prompted the Indian to address me directly saying they had previously been invited to the Sussex home of the ex-Prime Minister of Ceylon for Sunday lunch ten days hence and he would be honoured if I would join them. I was delighted and flattered in equal measure. The Sussex home of an International Politician of this standing was an opportunity beyond my wildest dreams and – as it was Sunday – I knew that I had no other obligations. Noticing my willing acceptance, he explained that he would get all details of the train journey to me at the shop. In return, if I would let him know my arrival time at the station, he would arrange to have me collected.

The following Sunday could not come soon enough. I had had many interesting and worthwhile experiences since living in London, but the chance to visit the countryside for a purely social occasion was a welcome contrast to the routine of dancing and the shop. Not only this but the opportunity to dine with such an eminent politician was the stuff of dreams.

The train journey to Sussex was uneventful except that I was somewhat surprised to find the Indian gentleman himself had decided to meet me with a chauffeur driven Rolls Royce. I would have thought the driver could have spotted me himself at this empty country railway station but, putting negative musings to the back of my mind I went forward and shook his hand. What happened as we both got into the back of the car left me surprised, a little frightened and angry – in that order – as he turned to me in a curt, unfriendly voice and said: "your face is too shiny, put some powder on."

I was stunned. How dare this man speak to me in this way. I had taken particular care before travelling to look my very best for the day and knew his remark was fatuous as well as insulting. Options crowded my mind. I was angry enough to get out of the car and walk back to the station, but my polite instincts prevailed, and I dutifully dabbed my nose as we made the short journey to a country mansion of breath-taking proportions.

My second irritation surfaced when I became aware that Elizabeth and Mary had *not* been invited. Back in London when this lunch invitation was mooted, he had definitely said *they* had been asked to the meal and would I care to join *them* in Sussex.

The ex-Prime Minister accompanied by his gracious wife and two adult children hosted the lunch at which more than twenty people sat at the table. The annoyance I had felt at the hostile greeting when I arrived at the station soon melted in the face of an extraordinary lunch table which was dressed with more complimentary dishes than I could count. Our host proudly declaimed that he had brought his favourite chef with him when he moved from Ceylon to England and we were to experience the best of his skills by joining in this feast. A long, leisurely and truly satisfying lunch culminated in people leaving the table in twos and threes to wander around the house and manicured gardens. The many rooms were superbly furnished, and each was worthy of scrutiny.

I found myself alone at an occasional table enjoying a flavoursome and satisfying coffee when I was joined by the Indian who was responsible for my presence at this memorable Sunday lunch. After a few pleasantries, he leaned in towards me and revealed his real reason for the attention he had paid me since our initial meeting in London.

"Now, you must listen carefully. You can see how happy Elizabeth and Mary are in London. I look after every one of their needs, and I could do the same for you. You have a successful dancing career, and I have learned your shop is thriving. I want you to move into the house along with them. All of your earnings will come to the house, and I will take charge of your chequebook. Believe me, when you think about it, you will be relieved not to have the obligation of bills to pay and other distractions. I will take care of everything."

He paused to study my face and assess my reaction. It is not often I am lost for words, but this was such an occasion. I was a long way from the comfort and security of my London home, and I suddenly felt defenceless and lonely, but my contempt for his crude attempt to induct me into some weird commune boiled over in a manner I had never before experienced.   Keeping my voice low, I hissed my distaste for him and his shabby behaviour.   If I were not returned to the station without delay, then he would witness a scene which would certainly ensure he would never be welcome in this part of Sussex again. His face took on a brutal expression, and I was shaking with fear, but the car appeared, and I returned to London without incident.

I never saw him after this weekend, and I often wondered what actually went on in that elegant house on the edge of Regents Park?

16

The 'Honey-Trap.'

In the 60's and 70's when the Cold War still menaced Western Countries, the British Government commissioned several 'cinema quality' training films designed to highlight the dangers The Armed Forces faced from an enemy determined to capture secret information. Contracts for such films were placed with the BIFP (British Institute of Film Producers) who commissioned some of their members to fulfil the requirement on a not-for-profit basis.

The script for just such a training film called for a belly dancer, and because of the significant publicity I was receiving, my agent got a call. I met the producer for an informal chat, and he readily declared his lack of understanding of acts such as mine. He was very considerate towards me, and I sensed that he would like some first-hand experience of my work. I was secretly very thrilled when he proposed bringing his wife to watch my performance at the Bagatelle nightclub the next evening.

My dance was received very well, and later I joined them both at their table for a drink. They were incredibly kind about my performance and immediately asked that I accept the role of a seductive nightclub belly dancer.

The film was intended as a warning to Armed Forces personnel and The Security Forces that irresponsible behaviour could easily allow an individual to become ensnared in a honey-trap which could lead to blackmail and other unfortunate outcomes. In this scenario, I was to be the 'honey' that got the unfortunate young Officer into trouble.

The Producer then asked if I could act? I briefly recounted the TV roles I had had in the past four years, but each of them had me performing my dance routine and nothing else. I hastily added that I was trained to be an actress as I had attended acting classes in Kingston.

The conversation became very animated, and he explained that he had decided to go back to his studio and rewrite the script so that I would not be just an exotic dancer but would act the part of the *central villain* with significant lines of dialogue. I was stunned and *overwhelmed* with joy but managed to keep a demure persona while telling him that I *was* prepared to undertake such a role.

The days of filming were just brilliant. We spent a complete day in one of the poshest nightclubs in Curzon Street filming the nightclub scenes. No problem there, since I was just reproducing the dance I had been performing night after night for the past few years. The only difference being that I was seducing one Officer in particular and not playing to the whole audience.

The script called for a bedroom scene where the seduction was to take place while a concealed Russian Agent photographed the unfortunate victim in my amorous clutches. Then, hopelessly compromised, he submitted to the blackmail by disclosing valuable National secrets. I was twenty-five and, despite my many show business bookings, was still shy and somewhat reserved. I made it very clear that a 'bedroom scene' with the actor playing the young Officer was simply not possible. The Producer, who by now was acting as my mentor as well as Film Producer, immediately agreed.

The scene in question was finally shot *in my own flat.* Some very decorous scenes were taken of me in my *own* bed and, a few days later, were spliced most skilfully with shots of the other actor. Honour saved all round and a budget overrun avoided by using my apartment rather than a hotel suite. Every time I went to my bedroom wardrobe after that I expected the swarthy Russian Agent to jump out again with his camera!

When the film was complete, we naturally wanted to attend a private screening to see how the finished project looked, but amazingly the M.O.D. initially refused our request as the film was classified 'Secret.' Finally, someone saw just how ridiculous *that* refusal was, and we were shown the complete film in a private Wardour Street studio. I have rarely felt so proud. My lines were clearly spoken, and the diction was clear, and I was secretly very pleased with this my acting debut.

*

During the third day of shooting, The Producer met me and said that a colleague of his at *Thames TV* was looking to cast a female lead in a Six-part serial for Children's TV and that he had recommended me. I still had film make-up on, but he told me just to put on a coat and go to Thames TV headquarters at Holborn.

I was shown into a busy room with set designers, storyboard editors and a throng of assistants viewing sketches on large tables. The Director spotted me immediately and ushered me into his office where we were joined by the Casting Director. The fact that I had left a *film set* to meet them was clearly very significant to them both and seemed to satisfy any curiosity they might have had about my acting credentials. The Director happily explained that he had seen me dance at an Embassy function the year before and also had hosted a dinner party at *The Tamarisk* restaurant where he also saw me perform.

The meeting was *so* positive. It was as if the Director had already decided that I was right for this lead role. I was assured that the part was mine. It was stressed that filming would take at least six weeks and would be on location in East Anglia. I just had the presence of mind to say that I would have to check my forward engagements with my agent and they acknowledged this requirement. As I left my legs turned to jelly. *A six-week series on National TV, a leading role, and no dancing*!!

I remember sitting in the first café I found, drinking coffee and trying to calm myself. My thoughts flew to the problems this fantastic opportunity would present. The shop. By now I had three or four girlfriends who were all experienced in *Sonya's Perfumery,* and I was confident that I could arrange a roster with them. Besides, the schedule generally allowed for weekends away from filming so I was sure I could keep an eye on things. From memory, I had two dancing engagements that were in the diary, and they would have to be cancelled.

Once more, though, I had to suppress the underlying anxiety which bullied itself into my mind. There was not a single person with whom I could discuss this fundamental change in my career. I was certain of my own skills and, of course, I had Actors *Equity* behind me, but this was a huge change, and I experienced a level of anguish that, later, had me visiting a private Doctor for a consultation.

For the moment, still excited but calmer I made my way back to the *'The honey-trap'* film set.

17

Wreckers at Deadeye

The first meeting of the cast of *Wreckers at Deadeye* was fast approaching, and I was finding it difficult to think of anything else. We were to gather at a beautiful country hotel in *Hurstpierpoint West Sussex,* and I set off once again wishing I could share this career milestone with a loved one. I had never visited Sussex before, and the journey gave me an opportunity to marvel at the green, lush countryside; such a contrast to my childhood home in Teheran.

The experience I was about to face dwarfed anything my previous TV appearances had required and, once more, I found myself trying to quell feelings of self-doubt. I wondered if anyone else arriving for this group familiarisation was feeling the same mixture of excitement and dread? I reminded myself that I *would not have been chosen* if I was not capable of playing the lead role in such a significant production. To settle my nerves, I re-read the script preamble which had come to me by post one week earlier.

It explained that *Wreckers at Deadeye* was a six-part serial to be made by Thames TV and shown in a six p.m. time-slot for children and adults alike. The story took place in the seventeen hundred's in Cornwall and concerned the activities of inshore pirates known as 'wreckers.' These lawless villagers had an encyclopaedic knowledge of the rocky coastline in their area and would use lanterns during stormy nights to lure unwary ships onto the rocks. Once the vessel had foundered, such cargo as was washed ashore was looted and stored in secret locations around the village.

I was to play the part of a Middle-Eastern Princess who was travelling on such a ship when it was fatally enticed onto some rocks. The following morning, I was found by The Squires Granddaughter and the stable lad, lying half-dead in a small sandy cove. It later transpired that everyone on board that ill-fated ship had been killed except for me.

The remaining episodes concerned Government *Revenue Men* and their efforts to catch the smugglers, and the increasingly desperate attempts of the wreckers to find and kill me since they realised that I was the only one that could prove their malfeasance.

Meeting the rest of the cast was a pleasure indeed! Everyone was friendly and relaxed with several actors mentioning that they had seen me dance in London. Johnny Briggs, who later went on to have a long career in *Coronation Street,* was someone I knew by sight. He was kindness itself when location filming began in Frinton-On-Sea and offered me many useful tips and encouragement on more than one occasion. Arthur White – David Jason's brother – was a stalwart of TV drama productions, and his avuncular kindness calmed me more than once when filming became somewhat tense.

The nature of the plot meant that I was several times filmed in a flimsy costume lying in shallow water at the edge of the beach. I was desperate to demonstrate my commitment and immediately complied with all of the Directors instructions. One quite chilly morning I was lying in the sand being gently lapped by seawater for the third or fourth time when I must have passed out because I next remember being wrapped in blankets quite high up the beach. There was much consternation from The Director and his team, but I was so anxious to please that I assured them I was now recovered and would they like me to go back into the water?

The Director immediately ordered that I be taken back to the hotel for the rest of the day saying that this scene would be re-shot the following morning. After that, the daily *'props required'* list had an item *"Brandy for Miss Benjamin"* and, indeed, it was always on hand afterwards if I was filming an outdoor scene. One of the other actors seeing this had complained to The Director saying that every cast member shooting outside should also be given brandy each day. He was severely reprimanded by being told that any time *he* spent a morning in the shallows dressed in an insubstantial slip, then *he* could have the same consideration offered to him. It was then I decided that I enjoyed location filming *very much indeed.*

There was one other unusual addition to the *props required* list, and that was – of all things – liquorice sticks. I was completely at a loss to work out who demanded sweets as a condition of their contract? I soon learned, however, that chewing on these sticks produced a very realistic set of black teeth for the pirates. This effect added great realism to their villainous appearance and had long been known to be more realistic than anything the make-up department could achieve.

The six-week assignment was very tiring but almost certainly one of the most enjoyable contracts I ever had. The series ran on TV as planned and I was very flattered that my photo was used for the full-page front cover of the TV Times weekly magazine.

Once filming was complete, I received a phone call from Thames TV publicity explaining that having distributed the Wreckers 'story' to the press, they had arranged for several of the Daily Newspaper photographers to visit me at nine the following morning so that they could obtain a suitable picture to accompany the article. I was ready very early and quite excited at the thought of a National Newspapers running my photograph to help publicise the TV series.

Lucky that I *was* ready very early because my bell was rung at eight-thirty by a very professional young photographer asking if I was ready for the 'shoot.' As I got into his car, he explained that they had decided to run me down to West Wittering for some authentic location shots. This was quite a journey, and I was grateful that I had arranged staff for the shop for a complete day.

We finally arrived, and he busied himself posing me with mainly 'English Countryside' as a background including me leaning on a style which he discovered quite by accident. He declared himself very pleased and said the first picture would appear in *The Daily Mail* the following morning. He returned me to my flat sometime after lunch where I received an anguished call from Thames TV – "why was I not there when the photographers called me at nine o'clock?"

My blood ran cold. What had I been doing all day? I did my best to explain everything that had taken place earlier and was speechless when I was told that this was an old newspaper trick. The Daily Mail photographer had 'poached' me before the others so that he could have an exclusive scoop the following morning. The ridiculous story of the need for me to be photographed in West Wittering was simply to ensure that I was out of London for six or seven hours thus denying any other Newspaper from getting a shot of me in time for the papers the following day.

I was completely devastated. I felt stupid and gullible. My trusting Assyrian instinct which tries to see the best in people was severely shaken, and it took me a good while before the humiliation of this deceit left me.

Amazingly, Thames TV was relatively relaxed and sent their own free-lance photographer to meet me three days later. He decided that photos of me in the shop, as well as a couple in nearby Regents Park, would illustrate 'Claire Benjamin' in the best way. Needless to say, the photographs which were finally published were hugely beneficial, but being tricked in this way left me even more convinced that dancing and acting were definitely a temporary phase in my plans for the future.

There was yet one more bonus of this nineteen seventies TV series for me, and that was the ability I had years later, to buy the CD of all six episodes. At least the Grandchildren could now see how *Nana Claire* used to earn a living when she first came to England.

*

This year proved to be a very eventful and lucrative year for me, and It began with an unusual booking to appear at an international Telecommunications exhibition being held in the grand ballroom of the Grosvenor House hotel in London. All the main industry players of the time, such as *Pye* and *Marconi* were there to showcase their latest range of products. I had been retained by *Pye* to dance on their stand at a pre-arranged time on each of the four days to draw visitors to their state-of-the-art products and would I check into their suite on the first day in plenty of time to confirm all of the arrangements. I had a busy schedule of dancing engagements every evening of this week, and so four extra fees were very welcome indeed.

To my astonishment, I was informed that I was expected to dance three times *each day* and that the *Pye* PR team had agreed to pay a fee for *each* appearance. This added up to a staggering twelve dance fees in four days. This arrangement, plus the evening work I was already contracted to do, made this the highest earning week of my career. *Happy, happy me.*

The arrangements on the stand were perfect. Pye, who were actually exhibiting complete TV studio installations, had arranged cameras and monitors to record each of my performances. The music was played through a sophisticated sound system and was simultaneously relayed to *every monitor screen* throughout the whole exhibition arena. It was no wonder, therefore, that crowds literally flocked to the stand to see the unusual novelty of a live belly dancer performing for them.

The next-door stand housed bitter rivals *Marconi* who had hired four girls in ball gowns to wander around their stand at set times. It was no surprise that 'exhibition war' broke out with Marconi playing loud blasts of music every time I tried to dance. I was not prepared to attempt my performance with this cacophonous distraction right next door and adjourned to the suite upstairs to make my point. Soon there was a clear the air meeting between the respective senior management, and it was agreed that both companies would schedule their 'live' events so that neither would overlap the other.

This was a very enjoyable and profitable adventure for me plus the fact that I got to spend a few minutes with the famous athlete/politician *Christopher Chattaway* who, as Minister of Post Office and Telecommunications in *Edward Heath's* government, opened the exhibition on day one.

*

This year was also memorable for my bookings on New Year's Eve.

I had a contract to dance twice each night at Edmundo Ross's nightclub for two weeks leading up to, and including New Year's Eve. My performances were at eleven pm, and one am, and this had been in the diary for two months.

A couple of weeks before the year-end I was asked to appear at a New Year's Eve staff party being held in The Cumberland Hotel Marble Arch. This was a deliberately *early* event so the staff could get home for their own individual celebrations and thus I was needed at one-thirty in the afternoon. This would not interfere with the evening booking, and so I agreed.

One week before the year-end, I received a panicked call from my agent pleading with me to agree to an early evening appearance on New Year's Eve in, of all places, Maidenhead – some thirty miles west of London. To win my agreement, she explained that the company were significant newspaper publishers and accommodating them would "help us all." I calculated that I could cover this booking if it would be early in the evening, and so stipulated that I could only appear if they agreed to a nine o'clock dance time. She called back a little later to confirm their acceptance.

Come the day, I left the shop – so busy on New Year's Eve – late in the morning and was soon dancing in front of a hundred or so very enthusiastic staff members of a company whose name I have long since forgotten. Back home to bathe my feet, have some lunch and prepare to drive myself to Maidenhead.

I arrived at about seven to give myself plenty of time to see the dance area and check the speaker system for my music. My agent must have laid it on very thickly about my schedule for this day because the organisers were embarrassingly grateful that I could fit them in and be the star attraction at this substantial and prestigious party. I later learned that the Company was owned by the famous Dimbleby brothers, part of a legendary broadcasting dynasty and that they controlled a string of regional newspapers at the time.

A *very* fast drive back to London saw me arrive at Edmundo Ross's club with five minutes to spare. What a day, but how satisfying to have achieved all my objectives without disappointing anyone.

*

Writing about 1970 gave me an opportunity to review my earnings for the year. Taken at face value, it could be said that I had made a lot of money but, It was another year of considerable expense. I had rent and rates of the shop, similar costs for my Chiltern Street flat, and all of Mum's utility bills and other 'incidental' expenses. Also, my sister Bella – now married and in Australia – had just given birth to her first child that she had chosen to call *Sonya*. I yearned to visit her and hold my newly arrived niece, but it was Mum – with her well-tuned histrionics to the fore – who demanded that *she* should see her first Grandchild.

The only solution was for Bella and Sonya to come to England, and so I bought return tickets for them both.

They stayed with me in Chiltern Street, and it was an incredibly happy time except that Bella showed a marked lack of enthusiasm to visit Mum in Kingston.

Late 1970 – we have been in England for ten years.

Bella - Firmly established in Australia and safely delivered of her first-born daughter.

Joseph – Living on his own in Shepherds Bush and holding down a job as a film editor with Michael Winner; something I had managed to arrange for him through a contact I had in a leading London studio.

Dad - So much has happened here!   He has now left Mum and has set-up house with a new girlfriend.   He has left 'India Man.' And is a bus driver around the Kingston area. He begs me for money so that he can furnish his new home and, after much agonising, I loan him the whole of my fee from Wreckers. He promises to pay it back in regular instalments, but I never receive a penny.

*Mum - Rages from morn 'til night about Dad and her wish to kill him if she could. Visits me in the shop crying that BT is going to disconnect her phone unless she can pay arrears of **one hundred and eighty pounds**. She explains that she often feels the need to call her sisters in America as they are the only ones who love her. This massive bill means I am forced, once again, to use the shop takings to bail her out.*

Message to myself: This *must* stop.

18

Search for the Nile & James Bond!

The 'Wreckers' publicity had a significant impact on both the quality and quantity of the work I was offered in 1971. And, apart from a busy dancing schedule and concern for the health of my shop, I soon found myself talking with the Director of a proposed six-part drama series. This BBC production intended to portray Sir Richard Burton's exotic and adventurous life while he searched for the source of the river Nile and I was to be considered for the role of his Persian mistress.

In life, Richard Burton was a fearless explorer who totally immersed himself in the ways of Muslim society. He studied both the language and all the minutiae that distinguished Muslims from other religious groups and became completely authentic in his adoption of the Muslim lifestyle. So convincing was this transformation - including insisting upon his own circumcision - that he successfully managed to visit the sacred city of Mecca and to take up residence in Medina. This audacious behaviour totally convinced local Muslims that Burton was not an *infidel*. So much so that he was awarded the coveted green turban of those achieving *Haj.*

What a man Burton was. He became fascinated by the sexual mores of Eastern Society and translated the massive tome *Arabian Nights* into seventeen meticulously crafted English volumes. Not content with this excursion into Eastern erotica he then turned his attention to an equally prodigious work *The Kama Sutra* which so appalled the sensibilities of Victorian England that it was suppressed and heavily censored for the remaining years of his life. Burton wrote many books which caused the censor to send for extra supplies of red ink, but this man was a unique pioneering phenomenon who undoubtedly found his spiritual home in Arabia.

The first episode of the drama called for his Mistress, a Persian beauty, to read the poetry of the legendary *Omar Khayyam* to Burton as he reclined on a bed of cushions. This needed to be delivered in flawless *Farsi,* which just happened to be the language of my education in Iran. So, the part was mine! Richard Burton was played by Kenneth Haig, who was at the height of his popularity. He was gracious and sincerely impressed that I could spout the lines without a pause. Another fine actor, Michael Gough was playing the part of *Doctor Livingstone* in the series, and could not have been more encouraging while I was there. He later found great fame as *Batman's* butler Alfred in the eponymous film series.

The narrator for the complete series was James Mason. What a voice this giant of the silver screen had. My efforts speaking to a camera paled into total insignificance when I listened to his relaxed but hypnotic delivery. His distinctive voice never failed to give me goosebumps, and I just felt privileged that my name appeared in the credits along with this doyen of international cinema.

The BBC was renowned as sticklers for accuracy in their factual dramas, so it was not too much of a surprise that an Iranian expert in the *Farsi* language was co-opted from the BBC Overseas Service at Bush House. He was present to monitor both the accuracy and pronunciation of my delivery. I do not believe he has ever earned a more effortless fee.

Next to come was an ATV production of a very successful series called *Hine.* The plot, not unsurprisingly was full of *International derring-do* between the established stars *Barrie Ingham* and the superb *Paul Eddington,* and, once more, I was a mysterious and alluring Eastern dancer. By now, I could pretty much play such a part in my sleep but the filming fee was very generous, and I got to work with the brilliant Mr Eddington, who went on to star in *The Good Life* and *Yes Minister.*

This was closely followed by a call from the influential and renowned agency *Oriental Casting.* They had been asked to find an 'ethnic' actress for the long-running Soap Opera *Coronation Street* and had put my name forward. I initially thought this would involve a trip to the Manchester home of the programme but was pleasantly surprised to know that they wished to see me in Granada's London offices.   Once again, I was totally impressed with the organisation of the casting department for such an established programme as *'Corrie.'* The Casting Director could not have been more solicitous and knew all about my work in *Wreckers of Deadeye.*

He seemed genuinely disappointed when he explained that I did not look sufficiently *ethnic* for the part they had in mind and that they were obliged to be seen supporting black and Asian actors.   For some reason, this polite rejection of my suitability hardly concerned me at all. Working in Manchester for any extended period would have put incredible pressure on my London based activities, and I was also beginning, once more, to have unsettling worries about my future.

I was now twenty-six and quite clear in my mind that no one would wish to employ someone such as me once I began to look older.   Again, I was undergoing a period of severe doubt about my life coupled with the extreme loneliness I always felt during these bleak times.   My dependable private physician *Doctor Bell* saw me in his Harley Street consulting rooms and was once more ready with considered and supportive words along with a course of mild pills.

I particularly remember *this* visit to *Doctor Bell* as I was able, for the first time ever, to tell another person of a recurring dream – nightmare? - in which I am performing my dance in front of an enthusiastic and supportive audience. The venue is like nothing I have danced in before but my music is playing beautifully.   As I take to the floor, my legs will only move as though I am struggling through waist-deep water. No amount of concentration will persuade my limbs to move in time to the music. I am aware of discontented sounds coming from the audience, and I begin to perspire. Soon, I am in full panic mode, and I jerk awake with a powerful feeling of fear followed by disappointment at my inability to please the audience.

Doctor Bell was certainly not a psychologist, but his thoughtful reaction to this confession raised my spirits considerably. He believed that the stress of my current lifestyle was promoting these dreams and that, as my life developed, they would disappear forever. I fully recollect walking from his consulting rooms back to my Baker Street flat and promising myself that things would have to change. I was not able to rely on anyone other than myself, and I would have to begin controlling the events in my life instead of events controlling me as was the present case.

I had hardly any financial resources and was forced to work to pay my way, and it was clear that I could not go on in the same way for much longer. Everything was not doom and gloom however as the shop was showing a reasonable level of profit and the steady increase in regular customers was very heartening to see. I began to believe that I could, with a lot of luck, consider the possibility of a second shop. This would be a very significant undertaking, but my confidence as a retailer was high. I had learned a great deal about prudent buying and balanced cash-flow, and my new Bank Manager was a welcome breath of fresh air. I felt confident that I would get a positive reaction if I went to him with a soundly argued proposition for a second shop.

Such dreams were consigned to the back of my mind, however, as another dance contract with the *Bagatelle Nightclub* appeared out of nowhere and my busy life resumed.

*

Not many months later I received a call from *The Barry Burnett Agency* to say that the legendary James Bond film Producer Cubby Broccoli was looking for a Belly Dancer/Actress for a new Bond film being shot at Pinewood Studios. I was to present myself there at nine a.m. the following Monday. Luckily, Sunday was normally a day off, and so I had the whole day to prepare for this rare opportunity to meet such a notable filmmaker. Early to bed with lots of facial moisturisers and an early alarm call for a relaxing bath and selection of my best outfit. Thus prepared, I started out for the interview.

Promptly at nine, I presented myself to the *Pinewood Studios* gatekeeper who had my name on his visitor sheet. I was asked to wait for someone to come and escort me to what I was certain would be the casting department. After a little while, a lady collected me, and In no time at all, I found myself in a well-appointed office chatting amiably to the great man himself. His completely relaxed manner and courteous attention to what I said had me completely beguiled.

He explained that a key scene in the film involved a belly dancer in an Asian nightclub who had concealed a vital piece of evidence that *James Bond* needed. The film was to be called *The Man with the Golden Gun* and was to star *Roger Moore*. He seemed to have so much time for me and after thirty minutes of chat astonished me by saying he would like me to go with him to the set where a major scene was actually being shot that day.

The film set was vast, and there was much activity everywhere one looked. When there was a break in the filming, Mr Brocolli introduced me to Guy Hamilton the Director and then to Roger Moore himself. Both were incredibly kind and spent a good few minutes chatting about my dancing experience. Christopher Lee – the Bond villain – then joined us and the warmth from them all suggested to me that the part was mine.

Back home I had to remind myself that such once-in-a-lifetime opportunities rarely came to fruition and, besides, I was booked to dance that evening at the Belgravia mansion of a Peer who was being feted for his Seventieth Birthday. I had to put out of my mind the fact that I had had a five-minute chat with *James Bond* and concentrate on giving my very best performance for The Lord and his guests later that night.

The following day Barry Burnett himself telephoned to say that I had not got the part. He assured me that they were very disappointed but that I appeared 'much too young and fresh-faced.' They needed an older dancer who looked more 'lived in,' as the script called for her not only to dance in the present time but to be shown in flashback ten years earlier and they did not see how they could regress me ten years and for me to still look credible. My disappointment was very brief. I was always a fervent fatalist who believed events, good or bad, happened for a purpose and this part, clearly, was not meant to be.

147

19

At last! A second shop

Another busy day in Blandford Street and, because I had no dance bookings that evening, I had decided to thoroughly clean and refresh the window display. The Marks and Spencer girls would always stop to see what new fashion jewellery I had, and I could be sure of several extra sales when this time-consuming task was complete. I had my back to the door when it was opened rather forcefully.

"Sonya! You must get to *Leicester Square* immediately. I have seen an empty shop unit which I am certain is what you are looking for."

This breathless exhortation came from Robin a cosmetic Company representative and someone who had supplied me at my shop since it had opened. He knew of my wish to expand and apparently had kept an eye open for me while covering his territory in London's West End. What was surprising was the urgency of his plea since he was otherwise the most placid of men.

"it is on the corner of *Leicester Square* and *Irving Street* in a brilliant position and I am certain will be snapped up immediately. Here is the name of the chap who has a shop close by and he has the keys."

I immediately phoned my friend Marianne who said that she could mind the shop and, pausing only to give Robin a peck on the cheek, I dashed to the address he had given me.

I introduced myself to the gentleman who was holding the keys, and he handed them over willingly. I promised I would have a quick look inside and then return the keys to him. To my surprise, he suggested that I keep them as I apparently seemed very keen and that I should approach Westminster City Council who were the Landlords of the property.

The property was very narrow but had an excellent eight-metre frontage, and I knew immediately that I could show a substantial amount of stock with so much display space facing the street. I sat in my car and tried to calm my excitement. After all, this was *Leicester Square* in the heart of London's Theatre and nightlife district. The rent would probably be totally beyond my means and, for all I knew, someone had already grabbed the lease.

Not forgetting the valuable lessons I had learned from my earlier years of retailing I began to think about both footfall and location. It was one thing to be excited but could I develop this shop into a profitable business. I began to take stock of my surroundings.

Irving Street was a short road which linked *Leicester Square* to *The Charing Cross Road* just to the East. It comprised mostly of shops each of which seemed to have an individual style. Next door to the shop I was considering was a specialist business selling a complete range of Military and Association items such as ties, badges, cuff links and tie pins. Across the road was a philately shop specialising in stamps and rare coins. Two doors along was *Our Price records,* a very busy shop pioneering the sale of discounted vinyl records.

The street had *character,* and I was confident that a new *Sonya's Perfumery* would complement the other attractive businesses that would surround it. Bolstered with these thoughts, I opened the somewhat scruffy door and looked inside. It was − not surprisingly − a complete mess. A wooden shutter covered the open frontage, and the gloom was only outdone by a rank smell of decay. Finding a light switch, I became aware of some wooden steps down to a cellar beneath. I had no need to use them as I could see the basement was at least a metre deep in polluted water.

Trying to remain optimistic, I estimated the cost of draining and dampproofing the basement plus building a glass frontage to the shop would take most of my savings. With a sinking heart, I made my way back onto the street and used a nearby call box to phone Westminster Council property leases. I was soon talking to an extremely helpful lady who offered to come and meet me at the shop for a chat.

Within twenty minutes I was explaining my situation to a very interested and constructive Leasing Officer. I confirmed that I could completely renovate the basement and install a modern, well-lit glass frontage but beyond that, there was little to offer. She told me that this unit had been a newspaper and magazine stall, hence the absence of an actual 'shop front.' When it opened each day, the boarded front would be raised to reveal a large counter full of periodicals and magazines. She added that some of the magazines were of the 'girlie' type and that The Council was not sorry to see it close. I began to feel that she would like to see a well lit and refreshing perfumery in its place and, thus emboldened, I asked what the rent would be. The figure she quoted was totally out of my reach, and I think my face must have portrayed my shock and dismay.

This very kind lady then asked me what I *could* afford, and I told her that I could manage fifty per cent of her figure. She thought for a moment and said that my commitment to upgrade the shop and its basement was impressive and that she would accept my offer by granting me a lease at half of the asking price. She could see my excitement and, in what I suspect was an uncharacteristic gesture, suddenly gave me a warm and encouraging hug.

Now my already busy life became completely hectic as a combination of my existing shop plus several Significant dancing engagements all combined with my new job as *Works Manager* for the *Leicester Square* project. Notwithstanding this pressure, I had rarely been so happy. Hard work had never bothered me, and I could now sense that a new chapter of my life was opening.

Thanks to a regular customer in my shop who knew of my plans for the second business, I was introduced to reliable and professional builders who began the necessary work immediately.   I located a reputable firm of shopfitters who designed the eight-metre glass frontage plus shelving for both the shop and the basement beneath. With everyone cooperating fully, it still took ten weeks before I finally was able to open the doors of *Sonya's Perfumery* number two.

Business was immediately brisk as tourists thronged Leicester Square at all hours. I quickly set up a camera film developing agency and this proved very profitable. I also became adept at accepting foreign currency and had a list of exchange rates by my elbow at all times. A typical trading day would see me managing to serve a giddying number of different nationalities, hardly any of whom seemed to speak English.   The occasional Iranian or Assyrian customers, however, received fulsome attention to their requirements and invariably left with broad smiles.

As I suspected, *Irving Street* was a small community in its own right, and I was quickly accepted by the other shop owners. Local policemen knew there was always coffee to be had in my basement and they became a welcome feature in my new enterprise. The contrast between *Blandford Street* and this new venture was considerable as the former relied, almost exclusively upon local residents for its success.   Here, however, the days bustled with tourists, and I quickly adapted the business to their needs.

Any ceremonial parade in the West End of London would mean sales of around thirty rolls of film. Tourists seemed to have an insatiable appetite for shampoo, indigestion remedies, plasters and the other assorted items frequenting a typical holidaymaker's toilet bag. These every-day things made for useful turnover, but it was the perfume and fashion jewellery sales which made this shop a success. I had soon identified the most frequently purchased sales lines and was thus able to devote the available display space entirely to them. Part of my learning curve was to discover that Sundays were often the busiest day and that remaining open into the early evening resulted in an undiminished flow of customers. For this reason, alone I was so grateful that I now had a good number of girlfriends who were very willing to help out at the shop and were pleased for the 'pin-money' it gave them.

*

Although the shop address was *'number one Irving Street*, it's window backed into Leicester Square itself and was thus prime real estate. For this reason, the residential flats above me were occupied for the most part by well-known actors and entertainers. Immediately above my shop lived the famous stage and film comedian *Charlie Drake* whose girlfriend often helped me out if I was short staffed. The flat next to him was occupied by *Albert Finney* and *Diana Quick* who quickly became very frequent customers.

The many and varied clients that I served through the years I ran the shop in Leicester Square would fill another book if I were to list them. Save to say that many were famous; a few were *infamous* and that some of them are still known to me today. Ladies would come and happily chat about their 'personal' medical conditions as though I

153

was a pharmacist. Tradesmen would come in and ask me to remove significant splinters from their hands and, more than once, I was bandaging cuts resulting from accidents that had happened nearby.

A quiet and exceptionally smart gentleman in his sixties would often come and wait for the shop to empty before he would approach and ask me for "the diamante earrings you are showing in the window." He would explain how much he thought they would suit his dear wife. It took about six months and several visits for him to finally confide to me that he actually was not married but that he did enjoy "dressing like a lady" in the evenings. Once this confession was off his chest, he was able to visit almost weekly to take my advice on eyeshadow, lipstick and – yes – *much* more diamante jewellery.

20

A Call from Franco Zeffirelli

By this stage in my dancing career, I was sure that there was little left to surprise me on the acting/dancing front. How wrong was I? An otherwise unremarkable month was punctuated by an unusually excited call from *The Barry Burnett Agency* telling me that no less a person than the celebrated Director himself had instructed his team to locate an expert in the art of authentic Middle-Eastern Dancing. Was I interested in talking to them? I had no idea what the requirement was but struggled to contain my excitement when I indicated my willingness to meet.

Another Mayfair hotel, another plush suite and, once more, a very polished trio of 'Zeffirelli's people.' They made it immediately clear that I was not being considered for a part as a dancer but rather, as a choreographer for several significant dance scenes in a huge made-for-TV film to be called *Jesus of Nazareth*. Once the impact of this extraordinary opportunity had registered, they began to make a presentation about the film, addressing me as though I were already a consultant to the enterprise.

I tried to absorb their compelling plot precis but, in truth, my head was spinning with the considerable implications such an unprecedented contract would have for me. The production was to be the forerunner of the popular genre of *'TV mini-series'* that we often see in our homes today. The scope – and budget – was simply vast, best illustrated by the fact that no less than *six* Oscar Winning actors were to be in the cast.

The outstanding *Anne Bancroft* was to play *Mary, Laurence Olivier* was *Nicodemus*, *Anthony Quinn* was *Caiaphas*, *Christopher Plummer* was *Herod Antipas*, *Peter Ustinov* was *Herod the Great,* and *Ernest Borgnine* was the *Roman Centurion* at the Crucifixion. *Robert Powell* played the part of *Jesus* and was to be widely acclaimed for his interpretation of this most demanding role. My contract was for a two-week location in the *Tunisian* town of *Sousse*, and I began to arrange a roster of my girlfriends who I knew could look after the shops while I was away.

The eight-part series, to be screened Worldwide, was the brainchild of The U.K. TV mogul *Lew Grade.* The senior member of the team meeting me made it clear that support for the project came from the highest spiritual level and that both historical and biblical accuracy would be the commanding principles of everything to be shown.

Somewhat apprehensive but very excited I made my way to the airport six weeks later for the flight to *Monastir.* I was immediately aware of several 'professionals' who were going to the same place, and I was soon chatting to some of them. As luck would have it, four of the girls I met were the dancers that I would be responsible for once filming started, and I was secretly very proud to hear that they already knew *Sonya* would be responsible for their choreography. I quickly came to admire these girls. They were beautiful and had lithe figures, but they were here for their looks, not for their ability as dancers. Each of them was experienced and saw this visit to *Tunisia* as 'just another job.' They were flighty and ready to flirt, but their good nature and sense of fun were certainly contagious.

When we cleared the airport, there were several taxis available, but an unshaven man with few remaining teeth directed me to a scruffy taxi *on my own* while the girls piled into a second car. I was horrified. All my instincts told me that a solo journey in this unsophisticated country was ill-advised, and I began to resist the driver's gestures for me to get in. By now I was thoroughly frightened and cast around for a way to extricate myself from an increasingly tense stand-off when a distinctive baritone voice asked if he could join me on my journey to *Sousse*. The owner of the voice and also a wonderfully courteous gentleman was *Robert Beatty* a famous film actor at the time, well known for the rich tone of his Canadian delivery. I blurted my thanks and tried to explain my somewhat juvenile aversion to shabby, unshaven taxi drivers. Rather than chide me for my naivety, he urged me never to be persuaded alone into a similar vehicle in such countries, which gentle approval of my actions, did much to restore my comfort.

He was also making for the film set and told me he was to play the part of *Proculus.* This experienced and distinguished film actor shared some insights about

Zeffirelli and his style when directing films. I well remember him telling me that he was a 'large canvass' cinematographer; that is to say, he would accept no limitations to ambition in his effort to achieve the 'perfect' scene.

I was no stranger to Summer heat as temperatures in Iran could often reach very high readings, but nothing prepared me for the overwhelming heat that welcomed us that day. The sensation as I stepped out of the plane was akin to that of opening an oven door to check the family roast. So this was midday sun North African style? The few minutes spent standing at the taxi rank had left me scorched under a ferocious sun which dazzled everything beneath it in a way I had never seen before. Thankfully, the hotel was comfortable and air-conditioned, and I was able to cool down and collect my thoughts.

Most of the film sets were in and around Sousse and easily reached by studio cars they would send for me. There was little to do for the first few days, but The Director had called for me to be present, no doubt to absorb the atmosphere of this biblical epic. It was then that I rediscovered my lifelong love of *Backgammon,* for this was how I passed the time with Robert Powell during the seemingly endless periods of inactivity. This compelling board game was universally popular among Assyrians, and I had been playing it from a very young age. I must say that playing *Jesus* at *backgammon* was not exactly what you would call an everyday event, but I fancy I won more games than I lost.

Into the second week and I had still not been required to choreograph the dancers. I was not entirely surprised since all the talk at the catering vans concerned the subject of delays. *The catering vans!* Each vehicle heaving with exclusively Italian food delicacies. Even those of the cast not called to the set would nevertheless find their way to these vans for the exquisite food they offered. Such extravagance was yet one more sign of Zeffirelli's power as a World-class Director.

With only four days remaining, I attended a meeting where the production manager told me he needed me to stay for a further two weeks. In one respect, this was good news since my daily fee was very generous and it had just *doubled*. More worryingly, though, I immediately thought about my shops and began some frantic calls to arrange further cover with my friends in London.

Days of inactivity passed slowly now. I had visited the famous Camel market and marvelled at these magnificent creatures being bought and sold. I had also visited *Kairouan* the fourth most sacred city after *Jerusalem, Mecca,* and *Medina.* This last excursion entailed a forty-minute coach trip into *The Sahara desert* to view *The Great Mosque* of Kairouan– the largest holy building in the whole of the African continent. Here I saw substantial rooms stacked from floor to ceiling with hand-made mid-size carpets. There were many hundreds of them on view, and our guide explained that every female child in *Kairouan* had to complete and donate such an item before they reached the age of sixteen. While visiting this most sacred city, I actually believed that I had stepped back into biblical times as nothing I saw there hinted at an existence later than the time of *Mohammad*. This one visit above all has stayed with me long after many others have faded from my memory.

My task on set was almost an anti-climax. I had rehearsed the girls several times, and they danced without a hitch. The production crew was apparently satisfied as was I and I was soon on my way home back to twentieth-century London.

When the series finally appeared on TV, the critics were universal in their praise of this epic piece of cinematography. Several declared that nothing like Jesus of Nazareth had been seen before or since and nothing like it may ever be seen again.

My return to every-day life in London on this occasion was somehow different. I had not really enjoyed being away for a month, and I began to realise that I missed my shops very much indeed. The daily interaction with customers, suppliers, and other local retailers was deeply satisfying and the commercial implications of running a business – although challenging – motivated me more than the *temporary buzz* of an acting or dancing assignment.

I had just had my thirtieth birthday and felt that now was the time to commit my future to my businesses. A third shop maybe?

21

And in Conclusion

If you have accompanied me thus far on my journey of recollections, then I thank you, dear reader. This concludes the story I wished to tell of my life to age thirty. A host of young pretenders have begun to populate the 'belly-dancing' profession, and their enthusiastic performances owe little to the classic dance style that was my watchword when I was asked to perform. I have been aware of this trend for the past couple of years, and my decision to stop dancing seems now to be entirely vindicated.

The history of authentic belly dancing is fascinating, and its roots can be found in early *Egyptian* religious dances as well as folk dances of *the Romani tribes* out of *ancient India*. Some of the rhythmic moves are even associated with body postures designed to ease birthing pains. The dancer's sole task is to communicate the inner emotions she feels as a direct consequence of the accompanying music. The best practitioners of this complex dance form were accorded great prestige throughout the whole of *ancient Arabia.*

The decision to chronicle my story has, in part, been driven by the wish to assert that modest success in life can be achieved with determination and self-belief. The improbable journey from shy Assyrian schoolgirl to minor celebrity recognition in London was made without any family support or encouragement. I bitterly regret not having had a Mum and Dad who would proudly applaud their daughter, and I am somewhat embarrassed that I did not dare to resist their constant pleas for money even though my Father always earned excellent wages.

My experience of fifteen years in England has left me a fiercely proud Anglophile. What a truly marvellous Country this is. The vast majority of the people I have met have been kind and generous, and my heart is full of thanks for those first friends who supported me when my family turned their face away. I believe the British justice system to be fair, and the support given to those without work is in stark contrast to that which would prevail in Iran.

As a young immigrant, I set myself the urgent task of learning English and did my best to assimilate myself into the British way of life as quickly as possible. I actually bought – and still possess – a book on etiquette and tried my best to behave in accord with its clearly stated principles. I believe this made my acceptance into the London social circle much easier than it otherwise could have been. How irritated I am, even today, to see immigrants utterly refuse to alter any of their ways and yet complain bitterly about being ostracised. This bigoted intolerance towards their adopted country is bound to leave them isolated and forever denied the pleasure of enjoying their life in this free and tolerant country.

Nothing, however, will disturb the all-consuming pride I feel in my heritage. Being Assyrian goes to the very root of my being. The culture of this once great nation is in my blood, and no amount of Anglicisation will rid me of the love I have for the culture of my birth. To this day, the ancient Assyrian language still provides the commentary for many of my night-time dreams.

My two shops are holding their own, and the 'Leicester Square' business is particularly impressive as it captures the vibrant tourist market that throngs the streets of this famous part of London.

My social life is comfortably busy as I find myself in a circle of friends where attending a party or dinner is not immediately seen as an open invitation to something more intimate.

Where will this life's journey take me now? Certainly, I am deriving significant satisfaction from my present situation but, in the back of my mind, I am beginning to ask myself questions about the future. Will I be content to be a retired dancer turned retailer? What other opportunities may yet remain undiscovered? One thing is for sure; I feel very positive again and less fearful than I have been in the past.

As often is the case, it took a surprising turn of events and some more unnerving coincidences for me to suddenly embark upon a new life outside of London. Not only a new life but an entire second career building an completely different and substantial business based in The Midlands. This is how events unfolded.

One of my friends in London invited me to a party where I was introduced to an Englishman of about my age. He was handsome and made me laugh a great deal throughout the evening. I confess that I was very taken with both his relaxed style and his English manners and was secretly delighted when he asked if he could take me to lunch the following day. Thus, did I meet the love of my life who, thirty-nine years later is still my treasured husband and best friend in the whole World? No words can convey the pure joy of spending one's life with a *genuine* soul-mate; someone who will share life's highs and lows with equanimity. I honestly believe that some partnerships are ordained by a Higher Being, and I have no doubt that we were meant to meet each other on that fateful evening.

With these thoughts then, I close my reminiscences of the first thirty years of my life. The next forty years were, in their own way, every bit as eventful and perhaps…….. one day I just may record them in print.

Printed in Great Britain
by Amazon